AF432294

Enter the Fight

A 60 Day Devotional on the Battles of the Christian Life

Noah Shaw

"I have fought the good fight, I have finished the race, I have kept the faith"

- 2nd Timothy 4:7

"The kingdom of God is built not by those who rest easily in Zion"

- Paul Washer

Table of Contents

Introduction

Many Christians are not fighting the good fight. They spend every day going through the motions of the faith, frustrated that their walk with God is not thriving, yet confused as to why this is. They love God and want to follow Him, yet struggle to pick up their Bibles, are fearful of standing up for the truth, have sin in their lives that appears to be unconquerable, and much more. Despite their deepest desires, their Christian lives are full of apathy and complacency. The aim of this devotional is to kill that complacency, emboldening readers with spiritual fervor and developing the understanding that the things of God truly matter above all else.

The title of this devotional is *Enter the Fight*, inspired by Paul's words to Timothy when he told his protégé that he has fought the good fight, finished the race, and kept the faith. Paul often compared the Christian life to a battle, fight, or race, and for very good reasons. To truly follow Christ will not put one on a path of ease and comfort, but the opposite. The Christian life is full of conflict. There is the war between spirit and flesh, in which our sinful nature seeks to overpower our desire to serve God and our pursuit of holiness. There is the battle for the truth, as lies are spread inside and outside the church, drawing people away from a saving faith in Jesus. There is also a fight against the devil, who though he is a defeated foe, seeks to deal as much damage as possible with the time he has left. Like many wars throughout history, this spiritual war is fought on multiple fronts. There are many Christians unaware that the faith contains these fights, that following Christ means entering a battle. I want to bring awareness to this fight and remind every reader that this battle can be fought victoriously through strength in God and reliance on Him.

Missionary and pastor Paul Washer said that "the kingdom of God is built not by those who rest easily in Zion." Advancing the kingdom of God and faithfully living for Him will never happen for those who desire ease and comfort. Throughout history, the men and women who have been used by God for great things are those who took seriously Christ's call to "deny [yourself] and take up [your] cross daily and follow me" (Luke 9:23). Friend, do not rest easily in Zion. There is work to be done. There is a king to serve. There are people who need the gospel. There are lies that need to be defeated and truth that needs to be proclaimed. There is sin in our lives that needs to be extinguished. There is a fight to be fought, a race to be ran, and a faith to be kept.

I had a strong desire to write a book on this subject, encouraging Christians to boldly serve God in all areas of their lives. When a friend asked me to write a devotional, those ideas were combined and this book was created. While this devotional was written to be consumed over sixty days, you can advance through it as quickly or slowly as you desire. Each day begins with a Bible verse or passage followed by a devotional related to the battles of the Christian life. The devotional content is followed by a few reflection questions designed with the intent of you focusing on Christ, examining your life, and discovering new ways to passionately live for Him. Additionally, there is a reading plan that will take you through the entire New Testament in 60 days, for those who would like to undertake that as well.

Thank you for picking up this devotional. It is a small work written by a man with no advanced degrees, credentials, or accolades, yet I trust that God can use this act of faithfulness in ways I would not expect. I pray that this book is able to stir up your zeal for God and encourages you to embrace the battle that comes with following Christ, emboldening you to enter the fight.

Many Thanks,

Noah Shaw

Day 1 - The Gospel: The Core Of Our Faith

For I am not ashamed of the gospel, for it is the power of God for salvation to everyone who believes, to the Jew first and also to the Greek. For in it the righteousness of God is revealed from faith for faith, as it is written, "The righteous shall live by faith" - Romans 1:16-17

The gospel is the core of the Christian faith. It is the heartbeat of Christianity. Without the gospel, the faith is nonexistent. Because of that, it is important that you understand the gospel and internalize it. If you are serious about following Christ, about fighting the good fight, you must know the gospel and know it well. Because the gospel is the center of the faith, the enemy works hard to distort the gospel and replace it with cheap imitations. This means that you must not believe in *a* gospel (false gospels are widespread), but in *the* gospel.

What is the gospel? It begins with the bad news that we are sinners. We sin against God and others. God is a righteous god. He cares about right and wrong and will enact justice on every sin committed. That includes our sins, meaning we face the righteous judgement of God. This is in a place called hell. Hell is where the wrath of God is poured out on sin, and where every human being is by nature destined to be. Luckily, because of His great love for us, God the Father sent Christ the Son. He lived a perfect life and died on the cross, bearing the wrath of God that we deserved for our sins. Because of His death, whoever repents of their sins and trusts in Christ as their Lord and Savior will have their sins forgiven and be saved. Through faith, their sins will be imputed to Christ, and Christ's righteousness will be imputed to them.

That is the gospel. Preach the gospel to yourself every day. It is the core of the faith and to live boldly for Christ, you must understand it. The gospel is the greatest news of all time. Our sins were paid for by the King of Kings and the Lord of Lords. Your sins are not held against you through the forgiveness the comes from Christ's sacrifice. What great news indeed!

Reflection Questions:

What is the gospel? Can I explain it in under 30 seconds?

Why is the gospel the center of Christianity? What would the faith become without it?

How can I ensure that I keep the gospel close to my heart and at the center of my walk with God?

New Testament in 60 Days: Matt. 1-2, Rom. 1-2

Day 2 - I Have Fought The Good Fight

I have fought the good fight, I have finished the race, I have kept the faith - 2nd Timothy 4:7

At the time of writing 2nd Timothy, Paul was under house arrest in Rome. He knew that his chances of being set free were practically zero. He was either going to die under house arrest or be executed. As Paul looked back on his life, he was able to say that he had fought the good fight. He was able to say with confidence: "I followed the call of God on my life and was obedient in serving Him." That is a powerful thing to be able to say. Paul does not list any moments of lapse in fighting good fight. There is no: "I fought the fight for 10 years, took a break, came back for a while, then decided to retire and take it easy." Paul was consistent. It was not during periods of his Christian life in which he fought the good fight, but the entirety of it.

We should seek to have minimal regrets when looking back over our lives. We should have the same mentality as Paul, who lived for God daily. He had no days off from serving the Lord. If you are a Christian, you should never stop running the race. There should never be a moment where you sit back and say, "I did the Christian thing, now it is time for a break." Fighting the good fight takes a lifetime. Remember that Paul only wrote these words when death was immanent, and nevertheless he *still* spent his last days serving God and living out His will.

It is easy to adopt the mindset that we are only fighting the good fight during certain periods of our lives. We fought as a college student, but we are no longer fighting now that we have a full-time job. We fought as a newlywed but are not longer fighting after becoming a parent. We fought when we had extra time to read the Word and pray but are no longer fighting after our schedules became full. Friend, never stop serving God. You should be able to look back on the past year and say, "I ran the race." You should be able to do the same for every month, week, and day. There is never a moment you are not a servant of God. There is never a day you are not fighting the good fight. There is never a day you are not running the race or keeping the faith. How you do so may look different in different periods of life, but you are always a servant of God. Live every day in light of that truth.

Reflection Questions:

What do I think of when I hear "fight the good fight"?

Do I view "fighting the good fight" as an occasional task or a daily call? Why or why not?

What are some ways that I can live out this call on a daily basis?

New Testament in 60 Days: Matt. 3-4, Rom. 3-4

Day 3 - Wake Up

Wake up from your drunken stupor, as is right, and do not
go on sinning. For some have no knowledge of God. I say
this to your shame - 1st Corinthians 15:34

If you do not believe that you are engaged in a spiritual
battle, if you do not believe that holiness matters, that truth
matters, that the eternity of those around you matters, wake
up. Wake up. Wake up. Kill your apathy toward the things of
God. Kill your indifference toward spiritual matters. Kill your
passivity towards Christ. Stop living your life as if the things of
God can be placed in your pocket and revisited whenever it
seems pleasing to you.

Many Christians are living in a dream, in a fantasy land.
They live as though spiritual things do not really matter, as if
their actions are not significant, as if God does not care how
they live. In this world of make-believe, Jesus is the friendly
sidekick to offer assistance along the journey, but nothing else.
If this is you, wake up. Reality is much more serious than that.

Wake up and realize that sin is truly evil, and it is
everywhere. The world's favorite TV shows are often nothing
more than excuses to show explicit content to viewers. The
world's favorite songs are dedicated glorifications of
everything that God hates. The favorite pastime of many
individuals is the sin of drunkenness. Wake up and realize that
your actions matter. They matter to God. They have
consequences for both your own life and the lives of those
around you.

If you want to follow God with strength and boldness, to
truly fight the good fight, you must wake up and realize that
living for God *actually matters*. There are many individuals who

profess faith in Christ yet live passively and indifferently toward God. Those individuals have not yet realized the significance of the faith that they profess and will live frustrated at the lackluster quality of their spiritual lives.

If that is you, if you are passive towards God and no longer want to be, pray for and seek understanding. Understanding about the importance of following God, the reality of sin's nature, and the reality that every individual has an eternal destiny that will either be heaven or in hell. Pray for understanding that living for God matters above all else. Pray to wake up. As you awaken to the sobering reality of things, your desire and zeal for the things of God will only grow.

Reflection Questions:

Am I living in a fantasy? Am I unaware of important spiritual realities surrounding sin, God, eternity, etc.?

Am I willing to embrace the discomfort that may come from "waking up"? Or would I rather be blissfully ignorant?

Am I serious about my faith? Am I serious about the things of God? What are currently my biggest priorities in life?

New Testament in 60 Days: Matt. 5-7, Rom. 5-6

Day 4 - We Will Give An Account

So then each of us will give an account of himself to God -
Romans 14:12

When we stand before the judgment seat of God, we will have to give an account of our lives. Of course, if we are covered in the righteousness of Christ, we know that we are safe for eternity. Nonetheless, God will still judge the quality of our lives. He will judge how we lived for Him, how we stood up for truth, how we shared the good news with those around us, and more. We can have Christ's righteousness, yet still live a poor-quality life, and will have to answer to God for it.

Many Christians lead lives that they would not want God to see. They ignore the things of God. They give a half-hearted effort against sin. They waste a lot of their time on trivial things. Imagine if God came down and asked you, "knowing that you are called to holy living, called to obedience, and called to share the good news with those around you, how did you live?" Most of us would be ashamed to give an honest answer.

For example, think of how much entertainment the average person consumes, whether that be TV, video games, social media, or something else. I would wager that if you added up the number of hours spent on entertainment per year, it would be a four-digit number for many people. Now, add up the hours spent on the things of God. Prayer would likely be a two-digit number. So would Bible reading. Sharing the gospel would likely be a one-digit number. What a heartbreaking contrast. This is not to say that entertainment is evil, yet for many Christians it takes a massive priority over the things of God.

It is things like these that we will have to give an account of. Now, it would be one thing if we were repentant of our spiritual laziness. Yet, many of us aren't! We are satisfied with our one Bible verse a day. We are content to pray only before meals, and maybe if we are stuck in traffic. We are content to watch our friends and family walk the path towards hell, unprayed for and never hearing the gospel. Heartbreakingly, most Christians will have to give an account to God for their indifference.

If you want to live for God, if you want to fight the good fight, it starts with knowing that God cares about how you live. He cares about how you spend your time, what things you pursue, and how you stand up for Him. We will all have to give an account of our lives on the final day of judgment, for better or for worse.

Reflection Questions:

How do I feel knowing that I will give an account of my life before God?

Is there any indifference in my life that I need to repent of? Do I need to repent of how I spend my time?

What will change in my life knowing that God cares about how I live?

New Testament in 60 Days: Matt. 8-9, Rom. 7-8

Day 5 - He Died So We Would Live For Him

He died for all, that those who live might no longer live for
themselves but for Him who for their sake died and was
raised - 2nd Corinthians 5:15

There is a common misconception that I find among
many of those who profess faith in Christ: the belief that the
purpose of salvation is an improved quality of life. You trade
a poor-quality life of sin for a high-quality life of freedom.
Under this mindset, life is still all about me, even after coming
to the cross. Life after salvation is effectively the same, but
with God as my personal assistant and sidekick as I live life.

This is one of the greatest lies stopping Christians from
making a major impact on the world. Friend, if you call
yourself a Christian, your life is no longer about you. Christ did
not die so that you could live for yourself with an improved
quality of life. One of the reasons He died was that you would
live for Him.

The King of Kings and the Lord of Lords bled and died
so that we could be forgiven and escape an eternity of God's
wrath. If we have any sense of thankfulness for that sacrifice,
we should have a desire to live for God. Before we were saved,
we were living for ourselves, our own sake, our own glory, and
our own pleasure. That choice was one that set us on the path
toward hell. Christ saved us from hell, yet many still want to
have the lifestyle and priorities that were sending us to hell in
the first place.

In life, you are always serving someone or something. You
are never 100% autonomous. There is always something that
pushes you to live and act in a certain way. You are always

under the influence of a higher power. You are always directing your efforts toward a specific end. In any given moment, you are either serving God, or your own desires. Your own desires are often sinful, irrational, and cause you act in ways that bring about terrible consequences. God, on the other hand, is not a cruel master. Serving Him can never go wrong. He loves you, He died for you, and knows what is best for you. Choose to serve Him today. Everyone serves something, but whoever serves the best master is the most free. Therefore, serve God.

Reflection Questions:

> Am I committed to living for God, or do I still want to live for myself?

> How has serving my desires created difficulty for myself and others?

> How does knowing the gospel and understanding God's character make it easier to live for Him?

New Testament in 60 Days: Matt. 10-11, Rom. 9-10

Day 6 - We Are His Workmanship

For we are His workmanship, created in Christ Jesus for
good works, which God prepared beforehand, that we
should walk in them - Ephesians 2:10

Here, Paul gives us a clear and succinct summary of our
calling as Christians. In the previous two verses of Ephesians,
he laid out the glorious truth about how we are saved by grace
through faith, not by our own works. There is nothing we can
boast about regarding our salvation. Yet, Paul does not stop
there. He does not write that we are saved, and then get to do
whatever we want for the rest of our lives. For Paul, salvation
in Christ was not simply a means of hell insurance.
Immediately after writing about our salvation, he writes of our
calling in light of our salvation.

We are saved by grace and subsequently called to do good
works. These works do not save us or contribute to our
salvation, but are a part of our calling as Christians. Friend, if
you profess faith in Christ, then God desires for you to do
good works. Paul even writes that these are works which God
prepared beforehand, meaning He has a desire and plan to use
your life. If you are a Christian, God has a calling for you. He
has a job for you. You have a role in advancing His kingdom.
Your role may be to be a prayer warrior, to serve in ministry,
to write music, to tutor children, etc. I cannot say what role
God has for you specifically, yet I do know that your Christian
life does not end at salvation.

Do not believe that your salvation is the end of your faith
journey. It is only the beginning. God has given you a holy
calling. Do not forget that we are servants of God and soldiers

in His army. It should be our desire to advance His kingdom. Knights to not enlist in the army to sit around. They enlist to serve the king. If your nation's leader gave you a task, you be eager would fulfill it to the highest degree of perfection. Greater than any earthly leader is God, and you are called by Him, the Sovereign of the universe and the creator of heaven and earth. The God of the universe has good works that He wants you, specifically you, to do. Will you pick up the mantle? Will you answer the call?

Reflection Questions

> Have I let my faith end at my salvation? Have I forgotten about God's call on my life?

> How does my outlook on life change knowing that God has a purpose for me?

> What are some good works that God may be calling me into during this current phase of my life?

New Testament in 60 Days: Matt. 12-14, Rom. 11-12

Day 7 - Put On The Armor Of God

Put on the whole armor of God, that you may be able to stand against the schemes of the devil - Ephesians 6:11

You are in a battle, whether or not you want to be. Upon coming to Christ, you voluntarily enter that battle. Pursuing holiness is a battle. Advancing the kingdom of God is a battle. Sharing the gospel is a battle. Put on your armor and fight. If you believe that the Christian life is supposed to be one of comfort and ease, you are wrong. There is a reason that Paul writes about the armor of God. He does not write about the pajamas of God, the comfortable sweater of God, or the street clothes of God. He writes about the armor of God.

And why do we need the armor of God? To stand against the schemes of the devil. You may not want to fight. You may not want to engage in the battles of the Christian life, but these battles will come to you. You cannot throw in the towel or give up. If you step out of the ring, the battle will follow you. Satan will not settle for your surrender. He wants your destruction.

In *The Pilgrim's Progress* by John Bunyan, the main character "Christian" engaged in a battle with Apollyon. He considers fleeing, "but he considered again, that he had no armor for his back." The armor of God has a breastplate, but that does not cover your back. The armor of God only protects you if you are willing to face the enemy. If you run and hide, you leave yourself wide open for attack. Spiritual victory is only obtained when you are willing to fight. Cowardice and fleeing will only result in inevitable defeat.

Many Christians are facing spiritual turmoil. Whether it is discouragement, feeling distant from God, spiritual warfare, or something else, many Christians can identify a battle they are in. Many Christians are losing these battles, though, because they are unwilling to fight. They put on the armor of God, then flee from the battle. The gear up for a fight they have no desire or intent to engage in. They are unwilling to fight for their relationship with God, to fight in prayer, to fight for healthy habits surrounding spiritual disciplines, to fight in general.

Triumph is not impossible. After all, we have God Himself on our side. Nevertheless, you will never win if you refuse to fight. It does not matter the quality of his armor, a pacifist is destined to be defeated. Do not be a spiritual pacifist. God calls us to fight, to be warriors for Him. He gives us His armor to face the real challenges that come with living for Him, yet we must be willing to face the battle at hand. Turning to flee will only guarantee our defeat.

Reflection Questions:

How do I feel knowing I am called to be a warrior for Christ? Is it empowering? Is it scary?

What is my attitude toward the battles of the faith? Am I headstrong, or do I desire to run away?

How do I feel knowing that the armor of God does not protect my back? Will that change how I live for God?

New Testament in 60 Days: Matt. 15-16, Rom. 13-14

Day 8 - Seek The Approval Of God

For am I now seeking the approval of man, or of God? Or am I trying to please man? If I were trying to please man, I would not be a servant of Christ - Galatians 1:10

Paul had gotten into much controversy over the gospel, particularly with the church in Galatia. The Judaizers in Galatia wanted to retain the requirements of Jewish law and hold others to those requirements. This was in sharp contrast with the gospel Paul preached, which created much conflict. Standing by the truth that we are justified by grace alone through faith alone brought Paul a lot of criticism. In light of this controversy, he asserts that he works for the approval of God, not for man.

That is a question that all Christians must ask themselves: who do you desire to please? As you live your life, who are you trying to make happy? Is pleasing your family a goal of yours? Do you want to make a good impression on your boss? Are you trying to accumulate as many accolades as possible? Pleasing others is not inherently evil but should never take precedent over pleasing God.

Many Christians will declare that they want to serve God and be used to advance His kingdom yet live for the approval of man. Friend, your priorities cannot be split. Pleasing God will often result in displeasing men. Pleasing men will often result in displeasing God. If our actions are motivated by pleasing others rather than God, we will only live for God when others approve.

Paul would have been a useless Christian if his primary concern was pleasing men. He would have failed to preach the truth when needed. He would have caved on moral issues and supported sin. He would have likely indulged in sin to become more popular among others. It was his unwavering devotion to pleasing God that made him the mighty warrior for the kingdom that he was.

As we live this life, as we fight the good fight, let us seek the approval of God above all else. When the most important question to us is "does this please God," we will be prepared to serve Him well.

Reflection Questions:

Which do I seek more: the approval of man or God?

What are some areas in my life where I strongly desire the approval of others?

What are some instances in which I have compromised on my faith in order to receive the approval of others?

How does knowing the value of God's approval help me follow Him in my day-to-day life?

New Testament in 60 Days: Matt. 17-18, Rom. 15-16

Day 9 - Do Not Become Entangled

No soldier gets entangled in civilian pursuits, since his aim is to please the one who enlisted him - 2nd Timothy 2:4

When a soldier serves in the army, their focus is on their job. Their service requires full devotion and attention. A soldier cannot have his priorities split between his service and a side business, his service and farming crops, his service and pursuing higher education. If he was, then his military service would greatly suffer. Likewise, as Christians, our attention cannot be split. This is not to say that Christians cannot run a business, pursue education, or have hobbies. Rather, it is to say that nothing should hinder our service to God. Our aim is to serve and please God. More than making money, developing a reputation, or winning the approval of man, our ultimate goal is to serve God. Removing the military analogy from today's verse, we could say that "no Christian gets entangled in worldly pursuits, since their aim is to please God who saved them."

It is important to note how Paul uses the word "entangled" to describe what civilian pursuits do to soldiers. Similar to being trapped in a net, civilian pursuits would entangle the solider, inhibit his movement, and prevent him from serving well. The civilian pursuits would not be a slight distraction the soldier, slow him down a little bit, or give him a small stumble. They would entangle him. Christians should view the things of the world in a similar light. Worldly things will rarely be a minor distraction to serving God. They will be a major distraction, a powerful obstacle that inhibits us. They will entangle us until we are stuck in the net of worldliness, unable to serve God with any real effectiveness.

Christians who prioritize fame eventually forsake Christ in order to maintain a public image. Christians who prioritize money eventually disregard the Sabbath or engage in unethical business practices to gain more wealth. Christians who prioritize fun will soon ignore the things of God and use that time for pleasure and enjoyment. Any prioritization of worldly things will inevitably lead to the abandonment of God. Things such as money, hobbies, friends, etc., are good things and gifts from God. Yet, anything placed above God will soon become an idol that demands all of our worship, energy, and attention. If you are serious about following God, about running the race set before you, avoid entanglement in worldly pursuits. Like a soldier, order your life in such a way that nothing inhibits your service.

Reflection Questions:

Is my focus primarily on the things of God? If not, what am I focused on?

What is my attitude towards worldly things and the pursuit of them? Do I understand their capacity to drive me away from God?

Have I let otherwise good things become idols in my life that pull me away from God?

New Testament in 60 Days: Matt. 19-21, 1st Cor. 1-2

Day 10 - You Are A Royal Priesthood

But you are a chosen race, a royal priesthood, a holy nation, a people for His own possession, that you may proclaim the excellencies of Him who called you out of darkness into His marvelous light - 1st Peter 2:9

You are a royal priest. Yes, you. This may seem like a big shock. After all, being royalty would place one in the highest class of society. Similarly, priests were the people of Israel specifically dedicated to the service of God. To combine both royalty and the priesthood would create a very exalted class of individuals. To put every Christian is such class may come across as too much. Is it true that every Christian is a royal priest in the kingdom of God? Yes, it is. You are a part of the royal priesthood. Whether you are a college student, a mechanic, a stay-at-home mom, a government leader, or a waiter, every Christian is given this outstanding title of royal priest.

Being a royal priest provides us with two things: great status and great responsibility. The great status comes from the fact that we are adopted into the family of God. This is not status in the worldly sense. It does not mean that we are better than other people, more righteous than others, more talented or more gifted. It simply means that we are a child of the King of Kings and the Lord of Lords. God reigns supreme over His created world, and if you profess Christ as your Lord and Savior, then you are His child. That makes us royalty. No matter what the world may say about us, the harmful words others may say, or how we may put ourselves down, we are still royalty.

Yet, being a priest gives us a high responsibility. In the Old Testament, priests were responsible for a lot. They were dedicated to serving God, communing with Him, and being positive spiritual influences on the nation of Israel. That is a responsibility that we have as well. While not everyone is called into vocational ministry, all of us are called to serve God, have a relationship with Him, and share Christ with those around us. Peter says that we are called to "proclaim the excellencies of Him who called you out of darkness into His marvelous light." As a priest, you are called to proclaim the gospel, to shine the light of God in a dark world. You may think that this is only for those with a special ministerial role, but don't forget, you too are given the title of priest, and a royal one at that.

Reflection Questions:

How does it feel to know that I am royalty, adopted by the King of the universe? Does that change how I view myself? What about how I view other Christians?

How does it feel to know that I am a priest? Is that a role I am eager to fulfill, or one that seems too burdensome?

How have I previously viewed serving God? Does my role as a royal priest change that?

New Testament in 60 Days: Matt. 22-23, 1st Cor. 3-4

Day 11 - Speak To Please God

But just as we have been approved by God to be entrusted with the gospel, so we speak, not to please man, but to please God who tests our hearts - 1st Thessalonians 2:4

If you are a Christian, you have personally been entrusted with the greatest message in the world. You have been entrusted with the gospel, the declaration that Christ lived, died, and rose again, so that all who repent and trust in Him will be saved. It is an honor, a joy, and a serious responsibility.

When we speak the truth, we should not do so in order to make man happy. Man is sinful and by nature opposed to the things of God. Why would we ever tailor our message to appease those who are against God? Paul commands us to speak in a way that would please God. When we share the truth, we should not focus on whether or not mankind will like our message. We already know they will not. We are telling them that they are a sinner destined for hell and in need of savior. We should be focused on whether or not God would be pleased with us. Our first responsibility in sharing the gospel is not to others, but to God.

Are we handling the truth well? Are we communicating it well? Are we speaking in a manner that God would approve of? God is not pleased when we twist and distort the truth in order to appeal to mankind. He is not pleased when we present a false gospel that will fall better on sinful ears. Our work as Christians will not be measured by how much we please people, how many individuals we can make happy, or even how many converts we make, but by our faithfulness to God.

The prophets of God, those heroes of the Old Testament that we look up to, that we quote, that often have entire books of the Bible dedicated to them, were hated by others. Their message was unpopular and despised. False prophets often rose up to counter them and provide a sweeter sounding message. If the prophets had wanted to make their message appealing, to fall nicely on the ears of others, then they could not have proclaimed the Word of God. History looks at the prophets as faithful men of God, not as failures, even though their message was often ignored and rejected. We evaluate the prophets by their faithfulness to God, not their success or popularity. We would do best to evaluate our own lives in the same way. Faithfulness to the message of God far outweighs any joy that comes from the applause or approval of man. Though we may fail by worldly metrics, we can still succeed by heavenly ones.

Reflection Questions:

Have I been guilty of twisting the gospel, of obscuring harsh realities or downplaying certain aspects of it?

Does the approval of man impact how I speak the truth?

How can examples from the Bible encourage me to speak in a way approved by God rather than by man?

New Testament in 60 Days: Matt. 24-25, 1st Cor. 5-6

Day 12 - Run That You May Obtain The Prize

Do you not know that in a race all the runners run, but only
one receives the prize? So run that you may obtain it.
- 1ˢᵗ Corinthians 9:24

When an athlete competes, they do so with the intention
of winning. When a soldier enters the battlefield, they do so
with the goal of coming out victorious. When a musician
performs, they do so with the purpose of creating the highest
quality music possible. Many Christians today run the race of
faith as if they were satisfied with last place. They live as if
mediocre faith and mediocre Christianity were their goal.
There is little urgency or drive to the faith of many. Paul
commands us to live as through we were in a race, striving for
a prize. It is one thing to live the Christian life, it is another to
live the Christian life boldly and passionately. When we get to
heaven, we would all like to hear "well done, good and faithful
servant," rather than "mediocre job, semi-faithful servant."

Unfortunately, many Christians live as the semi-faithful
servant. They are not interested in running the race. They
would rather walk the race instead of run. Their goal is not to
live to a life devoted to seeking His kingdom and His
righteousness. Their goal is to have fun, live for themselves,
and pursue His kingdom if it is convenient for them.

It is very tempting for us to live as the semi-faithful
servant. We may view our faith important, but this is *our* life
after all. Wouldn't we want to focus on what we want to do,
and visit the things of God when convenient or easy? This is
why spiritual discipline is hard for many Christians: they are
not running for first place. If my goal is to serve God and live

for Him, I will make time for the Word and prayer, I will avoid worldly things, and I will run the race with boldness. If my goal is to do the bare minimum needed to consider myself a Christian, I will simply try to get by. Friend, do not settle for last place. Run that you may obtain the prize, and never settle for being the semi-faithful servant.

Reflection Questions:

Do I live the Christian life as though I were running for last place? Do I have any drive to pursue God?

Am I content being the semi-faithful servant, or do I want to be the good and faithful servant? What are some attributes of each?

How can I better remember that I am running a race? How can I live as though I were running for first?

New Testament in 60 Days: Matt. 26-28, 1st Cor. 7-8

Day 13 - Train Yourself For Godliness

Train yourself for godliness; for while bodily training is of some value, godliness is of value in every way, as it holds promise for the present life and also for the life to come.
- 1ˢᵗ Timothy 4:7-8

Nobody seeks to run a race without training. Nobody goes into battle without preparing. Similarly, we must train ourselves for godliness. It is important that Paul mentions bodily training, because training your body does in fact provide great value. Physical fitness increases your quality of life, lengthens your lifespan, keeps your energized, and much more. For many individuals, their life is greatly improved by a consistent exercise routine. It is in light of all these benefits that Paul declares godliness to be greater.

If bodily training can positively change your life, how much of a greater impact will training in godliness have? Like Paul says, godliness does hold promises for the present life. By conforming to the image of Christ, by having close communion with God, we become more content. The fruits of the Spirit abound in our lives. We better understand God's will for our life. We have better quality relationships as we are more able to show God's love to others. How does one train in godliness? There are many ways. Read your Bible. Develop a strong prayer life. Memorize the Word of God. Strive to serve others. Dive into Christian community. Seek out godly friends who will push you and encourage you. Not only does godliness provide these earthly benefits, but Christ promises us rewards in heaven for faithfully serving Him.

Nobody expects to build muscle after one day of exercise. It takes dedication. Through exercising on a daily basis, one builds strength, muscle, endurance, and much more. Like bodily exercise, growing in godliness does not happen overnight. You do not become an expert on the Bible after one day of reading. You do not become a prayer warrior after ten minutes of prayer. You do not become a Christian role model after following God for a week. Daily faithfulness to God is how you become the man or woman of God you want to be, and it is how you better train yourself to fight the good fight of faith that is laid before us all.

Reflection Questions:

What are some ways that an increase in godliness would improve my life?

Am I someone who seeks shortcuts when it comes to spiritual growth, or am I dedicated to growing through daily faithfulness?

What are some habits I can implement in my life to better train myself in godliness?

New Testament in 60 Days: Mark 1-2, 1st Cor. 9-10

Day 14 - Called To Holiness

For God has not called us for impurity, but to holiness.
Therefore, whoever disregards this, disregards not man but
God, who gives His Holy Spirit to you
- 1st Thessalonians 4:7-8

"Be holy, for I am holy." Those words were spoken by God to the Israelites in the book of Leviticus. That call applies to us today. We are not called to be sinful, but to be holy. We are not called to pursue sin, but right living. We are not called to lead a life dedicated to the things of this world, but a life set apart for God. This call is one of the hardest for Christians to live by, yet one of the most important.

We are warned that those who disregard this call are not pushing aside an ideology or worldview, but God Himself. That is a sobering truth that many Christians need to hear. If you disregard holy living, you disregard God. There are many who claim Christ, who profess faith in Him, yet have no interest in living a life set apart for Him. Those people are not genuinely professing Christ but are in fact rejecting Him.

In the Old Testament, the laws surrounding holiness were extremely strict. God did not slack in regard to His holy standards. In Leviticus 10, Nadab and Abihu were slain for offering God strange fire that He did not sanction. In 2nd Samuel 6, Uzzah was slain for touching the ark of the covenant because it was forbidden to be touched by sinful men. The only reason we can even go to heaven and be with God for eternity is because we are treated as righteous and holy through Christ's work on the cross.

Though we do stand forgiven in Christ, we are nevertheless called to lives of holiness. Many Christians believe that they are called to simply live slightly improved lives. Maybe watch fewer explicit TV shows, listen to fewer vulgar songs, speak fewer curse words. The call to holiness is not partial or relative, it is entire and absolute. This is also one of the keys to fighting the good fight. If you want to boldly pursue Christ, while you do not have to be sinless, your life must be entirely set apart for Him. Pursue holy living. Do not be content with simply being less sinful than the world. Aim to set your entire life apart for Him, and to live as He calls us to.

Reflection Questions:

What do I think about holy living? Is it a goal I have, or a command of God that I have brushed off?

How does God view sin and impurity? Does that change my own view about sin in my life?

Has my goal been to have "a little less impurity" or to live a holy life, fully dedicated to God?

New Testament in 60 Days: Mark 3-4, 1st Cor. 11-12

Day 15 - A Noble Charge

As for you, always be sober-minded, endure suffering, do the work of an evangelist, fulfill your ministry - 2nd Timothy 4:5

This verse is becoming one of my personal favorites in the entire Bible. Towards the end of his second letter to Timothy, Paul gives him this charge. It is almost like a send-off, a graduation speech, or final words of wisdom before Timothy is left on his own to pastor the church in Ephesus. While these words were written as a charge to Timothy, they are words that should guide our lives as well.

We are told to always be sober-minded. We must be mentally sharp and alert. As Christians, we cannot let our judgement become clouded. Drugs and abuse of alcohol tamper with one's mental state. To live faithfully, our minds must always be sharp to discern between right and wrong.

We are told to endure suffering. One missionary I know has a favorite phrase: "grin and bear it." There is no way to avoid the truth that we will suffer. When we serve God, when we take a stand for Him, suffering will ensue. The ability to endure will make the difference between a lifetime of serving God, and a series of small and abrupt tours of service that end at the slightest difficulty.

We are told to do the work of an evangelist. Evangelism is something that everyone is called to do. While we may not be called into pastoral ministry, to be a missionary, or to be a street preacher, all of us are called to share the good news of the gospel with those around us. All are called to be evangelists. Each one of us has our own unique sphere of influence, people whom we can impact unlike anyone else. Let us not take those spheres of influence for granted.

Finally, we are called to fulfill our ministry. This is a broader command, but still powerful. Fulfill your ministry. Do what God has called you to do. It is simple. Are you called to be a pastor? Be a pastor and do so with excellence. Are you called to serve the underprivileged? Serve them and serve them well. Are you called to be an electrician? Work as though God were your client. Fulfill your ministry, whatever it may be. If we commit ourselves to those four things, being sober-minded, enduring affliction, evangelizing, and fulfilling our ministry, then we can know that we will be serving God and serving Him well.

Reflection Questions:

Am I a sober-minded Christian? Is there anything impairing my discernment and judgment?

Am I willing to endure suffering for the sake of the faith?

How often do I share my faith with others? Who are some people in my life that need to hear the gospel?

How committed am I to fulfilling my ministry? Is there anything distracting or preventing me from whole heartedly serving God?

New Testament in 60 Days: Mark 5-6, 1st Cor. 13-14

Day 16 - Scripture Is Our Tool

All Scripture is breathed out by God and profitable for teaching, for reproof, for correction, and for training in righteousness, that the man of God may be complete, equipped for every good work - 2nd Timothy 3:16-17

God's Word is one of our greatest tools in the battles of the Christian life. As we walk with God and seek to boldly live for Him, we will need guidance. We will need guidance about how to live, how to discern truth from lies, how to handle difficult situations, etc. When we have a question related to the Christian life, the answer will be in the Word of God.

Let us look at how God's Word can help us. 2nd Timothy says it is useful for teaching, helping us learn what we need to know. It is useful for reproof, helping us counter lies that others may believe. It is useful for correction, guiding us back to the right path when we are going astray. Finally, it is useful for training in righteousness, building us up to be great men and women of God who live for Him and are equipped for every good work.

I have witnessed many Christians have a low view of Scripture. They view it as godly words, but not as God's Word. They may believe that it has some useful things to say, but not that it truly came from God or that it can powerfully speak into their lives. Please realize that the God of the universe spoke and continues to speak through His Word. It is the voice of God in written form, and when God speaks, we would do best to listen.

Friends, we cannot fight the good fight without God's Word. We cannot be bold in the Christian life without a deep understanding of what God has revealed to us in the Bible. Many Christians try to do it. Many believe that they do not need the Bible, that they can navigate the battlefield without a map, relying on their gut instinct and intuition. Without a map, you will not get far. No soldier enters a battle not knowing where he is or where he should go. If he did that, he would be left to wander in circles, prime to be destroyed by the enemy. Likewise, Christians cannot fight the good fight without a map letting us know where we are and where we should go. That map is the Word of God, which is bound to teach us, reprove us, correct us, and train us if we dedicate ourselves to understanding what God has revealed.

Reflection Questions

How much do I value the Word of God in my life?

Have I pursued His Word for guidance when I have needed it? Why or why not?

How can God's Word help me better live for Him?

What are some habits I want to form surrounding His Word?

New Testament in 60 Days: Mark 7-9, 1st Cor. 15-16

Day 17 - Ambassadors For Christ

Therefore, we are ambassadors for Christ, God making His appeal through us. We implore you on behalf of Christ, be reconciled to God - 2nd Corinthians 5:20

One of your jobs as a Christian is to be an ambassador for Christ. Earthly ambassadors are sent by a government to a foreign country to represent a country and its leader. As ambassadors for Christ, we are living in a place that is not our eternal home. It is our job to be ambassadors for Christ to those around us.

Typically, the role of ambassador is very prestigious. You are *the* representative for your nation. The relationship between the foreign nation and yours is often reliant on what you do. To be an ambassador is indeed a special honor. That is an honor we have as well. We are sent as representatives to the world around us. You cannot refuse this job. You cannot tell God: "I do not want to be your ambassador." Your King has called you to this role. Embrace it. The King of the universe has sent ambassadors into a rebellious world, to announce His rule and His offer of forgiveness for those who will accept it. It is our job to make that announcement.

You do not have to be a minister to be an ambassador for Christ. You do not need an advanced degree, or specialized training. You are an ambassador in the workplace. You are an ambassador in your family. You are an ambassador among your friends. Just like how earthly ambassadors are sent to specific nations of the world, you are called to the areas of the world in which you currently reside.

As an ambassador for Christ, what must you do? Well, you must first understand and be able to articulate the gospel. Secondly, as a representative of Christ, you must also live a life worthy of the calling that you have received, representing Christ in how you live. Thirdly, you must do your job as an ambassador and proclaim the message of the King to those around you. It is no doubt a difficult task, yet Christ will empower you to live out this noble calling.

Reflection Questions:

How do I feel knowing that I am an ambassador for Christ? Does that change how I view myself, or how I view my life?

Is this a role that I am excited to embrace, timid to embrace, or unwilling to embrace? Why?

Am I prepared to be an ambassador for Him? If not, what are some things I can do to prepare?

New Testament in 60 Days: Mark 10-11, 2nd Cor. 1-2

Day 18 - Make The Most Of Every Opportunity

Look carefully then how you walk, not as unwise but as wise, making the best use of every opportunity, because the days are evil - Ephesians 5:15-16

There is an epidemic in the world of "Sunday only" Christianity. A Christian will show up to church on Sunday and joyfully participate in the service. Then they will go home and spend the rest of the week separated from the things of God. Through the week, they may occasionally read a Bible verse or pray over their meals, then head back to church on Sunday in order to repeat the cycle all over again. Their faith is often relegated to only one day a week.

If we are going to see any real change in our world, if we are going witness a move of God, that type of Christianity must be abolished. Paul calls us to live as wise, not as unwise. We are called to make the most of every opportunity, because we live in an evil age. All work for the kingdom of God must be done on this side of eternity. Many Christians waste the opportunities that they have every single day. "Sunday only" Christianity throws away its opportunities. It is unwise. It is unwise not to pray. It is unwise not to stand up for the truth. It is unwise not to hide His Word in our heart, that we might not sin against Him. It is unwise not to invest in other believers.

You have plenty of opportunities to serve God and advance His kingdom every single day. You can pray on your drive to work. You can read the Bible instead of watch TV. You can speak up for truth instead of remaining silent. When an individual is passionate about something, they will use every opportunity they get to pursue that passion. Those wanting to advance their careers will network with every individual they can. Those seeking admission into a specific college will spend hours upon hours fine-tuning their application. Those wanting to maintain friendships will make it a priority to keep in touch. When you have a goal that you truly care about, you do not mindlessly throw away opportunities. If we care about the advancement of His kingdom, about fighting the good fight and living for Him, we must not throw away our opportunities to do so.

Reflection Questions:

Have I fallen into the lifestyle of "Sunday only" Christianity?

Have I been taking advantage of the opportunities to serve God that have been coming my way?

What are some opportunities I have to serve Him that I have been ignoring?

New Testament in 60 Days: Mark 12-13, 2nd Cor. 3-4

Day 19 - Make Yourself Useful

Now in a great house there are not only vessels of gold and
silver but also of wood and clay, some for honorable use,
some for dishonorable. Therefore, in anyone cleanses himself
from what is dishonorable, he will be a vessel for honorable
use, set apart as holy, useful to the master of the house, ready
for every good work - 2nd Timothy 2:20-21

Here, we read about two types of vessels: those for
honorable use and those for dishonorable use. We are
encouraged to cleanse ourselves so that we can be holy, set
apart for honorable use. Friend, if you want to be used by God,
you must make yourself useful.

Many individuals desire to be used by God. Many
Christians want to do great things for Him, to passionately
serve Him and advance His kingdom. All the while, they are
vessels for dishonorable use. They lead lives full of sin, have
no discipline when it comes to the things of God, don't pray,
don't know His Word, and more. Now, this is not to imply
that God cannot use these people. God often uses those we
would least expect. At the same time, we cannot desire to be
used by God while simultaneously refusing to prepare
ourselves for His service.

We cannot expect to be prayer warriors without
developing a prayer life. We cannot expect to be strong
evangelists unless we know how to articulate the gospel. We
cannot expect to defeat the reigning lies of our day without
knowing how to counter those lies. We cannot expect to speak
the truth to others without being deeply acquainted with that
truth. These are steps we must take for ourselves. Mighty

warriors do not appear out of thin air, they are trained for battle. Mighty servants of God do not appear out of thin air, they are trained for His service.

If you are reading this devotional, you likely have a desire to be used by God. You likely want to fight for Him and advance His kingdom. That is an amazing desire to have, yet it is a desire that must be lived out. While God can use anybody, He tends to use those who want to be used. And those who truly want to be used are those who prepare themselves and make themselves available. In preparing yourself for the service of God, there is one attribute that is important more than the rest: faithfulness. If you want to be used by God, do not stress about getting an advanced degree, finding a platform to speak on, or defeating every sin in your life. Be faithful. Be faithful to prayer, to His word, to Christian fellowship and living for Him. If you do that, you will inevitably become a vessel for honorable use.

Reflection Questions:

What are some characteristics of a vessel for dishonorable use? What about for honorable use?

Do I have a desire to be used by God? Am I taking steps to prepare myself for His service?

What steps should I take to be more faithful to God? How will taking those steps better help me serve Him?

New Testament in 60 Days: Mark 14-16, 2nd Cor. 5-6

Day 20 - His Grace Is Sufficient

But He said to me, "My grace is sufficient for you, for my power is made perfect in weakness." Therefore I will boast all the more gladly of my weakness, so that the power of Christ may rest upon me - 2nd Corinthians 12:9

Paul had a difficult life. He was persecuted, hated, beaten, arrested, and more. His service of God was filled with pain and struggle. Famously, Paul writes in 2nd Corinthians about a thorn in his flesh: a messenger of Satan that tormented him so much that he begged God to take it away. It was too much for Paul. Maybe he could deal with being arrested and hated, but this thorn had driven him to his breaking point. It is in this context that Christ tells Paul, "My grace is sufficient for you." Paul could not do it on his own. He needed God's grace, and God's grace was enough.

Many of us have something in our lives that feels like our personal thorn in the flesh, something that stops us from serving God, something we believe is holding us back. It could be a stutter when we speak, extreme self-consciousness, or a habitual sin that we think stops us from ever being able to serve God. Each one of us has something that makes us believe we can't live for God. And that's the whole point. We are limited. We cannot do it all on our own. We cannot live for God on our own. We are imperfect, and something will always get in our way. Our thorn will make us think "this is impossible for us," and it is. Yet, God's grace is sufficient.

God's grace is enough to strengthen us and supernaturally nullify our weaknesses. That is why Christ says, "my power is made perfect in weakness." The areas in our life where we are weak, where we cannot do it on our own strength, are the perfect opportunities for God to demonstrate His strength and do much more than we could ever imagine. Friend, do not worry about your failings. Do not worry about whether or not you can serve Him in your own strength. You cannot, yet His grace is sufficient for you. Our efforts and strength will fail, but His never will.

Reflection Questions:

What is my "thorn in the flesh"? What makes me feel like serving God is impossible?

How often do I try to live for God on my own strength, to conquer battles without Him?

How do I feel knowing that God's grace will cover my shortcomings, that His grace is enough for every "thorn" I may have? Will that change how I view living for God?

New Testament in 60 Days: Luke 1-2, 2nd Cor. 7-8

Day 21 - A War Against Your Soul

Beloved, I urge you as sojourners and exiles to abstain from
the passions of the flesh, which wage war against your soul
- 1st Peter 2:11

The flesh and the spirit are at war with each other. That is
a fundamental truth of the Christian faith. The flesh wants to
indulge in sinful desires. The spirit wants to abstain from them.
The flesh wants to serve one's selfish interests. The spirit
wants to serve God and others. The flesh wants to turn away
from God. The spirit wants to turn towards Him.

It is in the context of this battle in which we read from
Peter that the passions of the flesh wage war against your soul.
I believe that understanding sin in this way would change our
entire outlook on life. We tend to view sin in ways that are not
so severe. When tempted to sin, we may rationalize that this
sin is "not so bad." We may excuse our sin by saying that "it
won't hurt anybody." We may jokingly say that everyone is
entitled to one selfish deed a day. Whatever excuse we come
up with, it is human tendency to view sin as something less
severe than it actually is.

This mindset increases the number of times we surrender
to our sinful desires. Temptation becomes a lot stronger when
we downplay the action and its consequences. Yet, what if we
viewed sin as Peter describes it here? What if we viewed every
sin as something that wages war against our soul and our
spiritual wellbeing? I believe a lot would change.

We need to change our mindset. We are not simply
"burning off steam" by swearing. We are purposefully using
impure words that God hates and training ourselves for

ungodly speech. We are not taking "just a little peak" when we do a double take at a scantily clad man or woman. We are indulging in lust and training our minds to be impure. We are not "avoiding tension" when we lie about difficult yet important truths. We are training ourselves in deception and feeding a distaste for honesty in our souls.

Friend, understand that sin is much more than you may initially believe. Sin is waging war against our spiritual lives and our godliness. If that is true, why would we purposefully indulge in sin? Let us heed the words of Peter and abstain from the passions of the flesh which wage war against our souls, yet never forget that Christ's sacrifice covers all of our failings and is why we stand righteous in God's sight.

Reflection Questions:

What do I think about the fact that sin is waging war against my soul?

How do I tend to view sin? Do I see it as something severely evil, or something that is only minorly bad?

What are some sins I have excused in the past, and how have they hurt my walk with God?

New Testament in 60 Days: Luke 3-5, 2nd Cor. 9-10

Day 22 - Put Sin To Death

Put to death therefore what is earthly in you: sexual immortality, impurity, passion, evil desire, and covetousness, which is idolatry. On account of these the wrath of God is coming - Colossians 3:5-6

Destroy sin before it destroys you. One of the strongest influences that will destroy your walk with God is unrepentant sin. That is why we are commanded to put to death what is earthly within us. We are not called to have a healthy moderation of sin, to keep it weakly alive. We are called to put sin to death.

Too many Christians try to live with sin in "healthy moderation." Just enough sexual immorality that is does not get in the way of relationships and day-to-day life. Just enough impurity to have fun every now and then. Just enough rage to experience a cathartic burst of anger when needed. Friend, there is no such thing as sin in healthy moderation. Kill it. If you are not fighting against sin, it will destroy you. You cannot call a cease fire with sin. Every day of your life sin is fighting against you. You cannot tell sin, "Only this far, but no further." It does not listen. If you give sin an inch, it will take a mile. Sin does not negotiate. If sin does not negotiate, then we should not either.

God hates sin. That should be enough for us to want to kill sin, to abolish it from our lives. We may enjoy a little bit of sexual immorality every now and then, but God hates it. We may have fun with gossip and slander, yet God despises it. Why would we want to keep alive that which God hates? Why would we seek a "healthy amount" of that which sent Christ to the cross? God the Father poured out His wrath on Christ, because of lust, anger, lying, drunkenness, cheating, fornication, and much more. Our sin caused God to put Christ to death. If our sin caused Christ to die, then we should want sin to experience nothing other than the same fate.

If you are truly passionate about living for Christ, if you want to fight the good fight, you must not allow sin to go uncontested. Repent of your sins. Call on the Holy Spirit for help. Pray for sanctification. Do not sit idly by as sin seeks to destroy you.

Reflection Questions:

What is my mindset surrounding sin? Have I ever tried to experience sin in "healthy moderation"?

Have I ever given sin an inch, only for it to take me much further than I ever intended?

How should God's attitude for sin, and the sacrifice of Christ, inform my own attitude toward sin?

New Testament in 60 Days: Luke 6-7, 2nd Cor. 11-13

Day 23 - The Fruit Of Righteousness

For the moment all discipline seems painful rather than pleasant, but later it yields the peaceful fruit of righteousness to those who have been trained by it - Hebrews 12:11

Christian discipline is rarely pleasant. Conviction from the Holy Spirit about sin in our lives is uncomfortable. Being confronted by a fellow believer can be embarrassing. Working out our salvation, killing the flesh while feeding the spirit, is difficult and often discouraging. Whatever form it may come in, discipline is never fun. Not only is our pride damaged by the realization that we are more sinful than we previously thought, but we must now embark on the journey of surrendering to the Holy Spirit as He reforms us and removes that sin from our lives, a journey which can be long and arduous.

Because of these factors, many Christians avoid discipline. They don't listen to the Holy Spirit. They disregard the counsel of other Christians. They refuse to examine their own lives. They just want to live their life, do their own thing, and not worry about sin. It would seem much easier that way. Life contains many burdens, whether that be paying bills, maintaining friendships, or working 40 hours a week. Who would want to add the burden of discipline on top of that?

Yet, as Christians, it is vitally important that we allow ourselves to be disciplined over our sin, whether that discipline comes from God, others, or ourselves. God's Word says that discipline, though painful, results in the peaceful fruit of righteousness. The result of discipline in our lives is peace and righteousness. It may be taxing to be disciplined over our anger, but the result is less anger. Not only does that increase our peace, but it improves our relationship with others. Discipline over sexual sin often involves struggle and discouragement, yet it results in a mind at peace along with better romantic relationships. Disciple over idleness and sloth is often humbling and requires an increase in hard work, yet it gives us the peace of knowing that we are truly living for Him and causes us to better serve God and others.

Friend, discipline is painful in the moment, but it will drastically improve not only your walk with God, but your quality of life as a whole. To boldly live for God, you must be willing to experience discipline. It is much better to accept the difficulty of discipline now than face the consequences of ungodliness. Discipline brings temporary pain but permanent relief, while ignoring discipline brings temporary relief in exchange for a lifetime of pain.

Reflection Questions:

What is my attitude towards discipline? Do I avoid it, or do I accept godly correction?

Do I view discipline as burdensome or worthwhile? Why?

What are some sins that I want diminished in my life? Am I willing to accept discipline over them?

New Testament in 60 Days: Luke 8-9, Gal. 1-2

Day 24 - Christ Was Tempted As Well

For because He Himself has suffered when tempted, He is able to help those who are being tempted - Hebrews 2:18

Temptation is one of the greatest struggles of the Christian life. In the battle between flesh and spirit, the flesh will always try to make sin appealing and will often succeed in doing so. One of the most difficult aspects of temptation is feeling like you are all alone. It can be heartbreaking to believe that nobody else understands, that nobody can help you or truly sees what you are going through. These feelings of hopelessness can often cause us to give into temptation when we would have otherwise remained strong.

Luckily for us, Christ understands. He understands the burden and pain of temptation. He was tempted by the master tempter, Satan, in the wilderness. As a human being, Jesus also had to face temptation in His day-to-day life. In fact, Jesus dealt with the pain of temptation far greater than we have, simply because He never gave in. When we are tempted, there is pain and tension until we either give in or the temptation leaves. Once we give in, the temptation goes away, which means that the battle is over and we experience some relief. Christ never gave in. He never experienced the relief that comes with caving to temptation. He faced the full might of temptation and never anything less.

This truth should provide us with great comfort for two reasons. First, it means that Christ can empathize with us. He is not looking down from heaven thinking, "foolish human, why do you struggle?" He understands the difficulty and pain that comes with temptation and can comfort us in that.

Secondly, because Christ has defeated temptation, we know that He can help us defeat it as well. We cannot beat temptation on our own. We may be able to fend it off for a period of time, but it will never relent in its assault. Luckily, we know the one person who has beat temptation, who has beaten sin, and He just so happens to be our Lord and Savior who we can call on for help anytime we are in need. In the battle against temptation, Christ is our greatest ally.

Reflection Questions:

What are some temptations that I have been struggling with recently?

How does the knowledge of Christ's temptation bring comfort to me?

How willing am I to call on God for help in the midst of temptation? Do I think He will look down on me, or lovingly provide help?

New Testament in 60 Days: Luke 10-12, Gal. 3-4

Day 25 - Instruments For Righteousness

Do not present your members to sin as instruments for unrighteousness, but present yourselves to God as those who have been brought from death to life, and your members to God as instruments for righteousness - Romans 6:13

We can sin with different parts of our bodies. Our eyes can be used to lust and to foster jealousy. Our mouths can be used to speak profanely and tear down others. Our hands can be used to steal and to hurt. Our minds can be used to think depraved thoughts. Our most intimate areas can be used to commit fornication, adultery, and a variety of other sexual sins.

Our bodies can also be used for the sake of goodness and righteousness. Our eyes can be used to read the Word of God. Our mouths can be used to praise Him and uplift others. Our hands be used in the service of others. Our minds can be used to think of creative ways to advance His kingdom. Our most intimate areas can be used to show love to our spouse in marriage.

While every Christian must make the choice to serve God rather than their sinful desires, to pursue righteousness instead of unrighteousness, we often forget that this choice is made with every part of our bodies. It is not enough to use most of our instruments for God's sake yet reserve one or two for the desires of the flesh.

Dedicate every part of yourself to the service of God. If you want to powerfully serve Him, to fight the good fight of faith, it will take every part of your body. If you allow your eyes to remain dedicated to unrighteousness, your eyes will be your downfall. If you carelessly allow your mouth to say whatever you want, you mouth will be your downfall. If you are not watchful over your thoughts, your mind will be your downfall. Whatever instrument of our body we fail to dedicate to God will be the one that consistently and powerfully drives us away from Him. Dedicate every part of yourself to God today. Commit yourself, every single part of yourself, to be used for righteousness' sake rather than unrighteousness.

Reflection Questions:

What sins seem to always reappear in my life? What part of my body commits that sin?

What boundaries should I set up surrounding my eyes? My ears? My hands? Etc.?

What would it look like to dedicate my eyes to the service of God? What about my mouth? My mind? My hands? Etc.?

New Testament in 60 Days: Luke 13-14, Gal. 5-6

Day 26 - Take Heed Lest You Fall

Therefore let anyone who thinks that he stands take heed lest
he fall - 1st Corinthians 10:12

Friend, be very careful that you do not let pride slip into
your sanctification. Pride says, "I have beaten sin and gotten it
under control." As soon as you think that, you provide sin an
amazing opportunity to wreck your life. Now, there is nothing
wrong with believing that you are less susceptible to certain
sins or appreciating how far you have grown in certain areas,
but you must know that you are never impervious to sin.

As soon as we believe that a certain sin is gone forever,
that we have vanquished it from our lives, we stop looking out
for it. Unawareness of sin is the perfect breeding ground for
sin and moral failure. I once heard of a Christian leader who
was asked "if Satan was going to cause you to fall, what area
of your life would he attack?" Now, most Christians know
their weak spots. They know that they are naturally more
resistant to certain sins but struggle more with others. This
Christian leader, though, answered the question in the
negative. He said "I know where he could never get me. He
could never attack me in the area of my family and marital
faithfulness." A few years down the road, this man was caught
in controversy because of infidelity to his wife. He ignored the
possibility of an affair, and it was able to take him by surprise
as a result.

King David likely never thought that he could become an
adulterer. If you told him at the start of his reign, "you will
murder a man after sleeping with his wife," he would have
called you crazy. Yet, he fell. Jesus told Peter, "Truly, I tell

you, this very night, before the rooster crows, you will deny me three times." Peter said to him, "Even if I must die with you, I will not deny you!" (Matthew 26:34-35). Peter could never imagine a world in which he denied Jesus. He didn't even think it was a possibility. Yet, he fell. Many people believe that they have permanently beaten sin, that they can never fall. When they do give in to sin after believing these things, they are often devastated.

Do not think that you have permanently beaten sin. You never cease to be a sinner. Our attitude toward sin must be one of constant humility. We defeat sin by the grace of God and must engage in the fight every single day. The battle is one that lasts a lifetime. Let us constantly rely on God for strength, knowing that through His strength and His strength alone, we can live a life of godliness. Let us avoid pride surrounding our sanctification and take heed, lest we fall.

Reflection Questions:

What is my attitude towards sin? Do I believe that I have conquered it?

What sin do I believe that I will never commit? How can I be on guard against it?

How can I foster humility surrounding the battle with sin instead of cultivating pride?

New Testament in 60 Days: Luke 15-17, Eph. 1-2

Day 27 - Draw Near To The Throne

Let us then with confidence draw near to the throne of grace, that we may receive mercy and find grace to help in time of need - Hebrews 4:16

We are not supposed to do this battle alone. We cannot serve God without His help. We cannot stand strong for Him without His help. Some Christians wrongly and unfortunately believe that God wants us and expects us to do it all on our own. If we struggle with sin, if we can't find the strength to stand for truth, if we are scared to share the gospel, many believe that God scoffs at us and says, "how pathetic, just toughen up and be better." They have an image of a punitive God who is upset that all His servants seem to be utterly incapable. Because of that image, many don't ask God for help. They don't pray for strength, or guidance, or wisdom, because they fear that God will view that as a sign of pitiful incompetence that should have been overcome long ago. This could not be further from the truth.

When we approach God's throne for help, we do not have to do so with fear. We are not told to approach the throne of judgment with fear and trembling. We are told to approach the throne of grace with confidence! If you have been saved, you have been adopted into the family of God. You are a son or daughter of the King of Kings and the Lord of Lords, and you are loved as such. You do not have to be scared to ask God for help, you can confidently do so.

This truth should empower us to pray and seek God's help daily. Whenever we encounter a struggle, we can go to Him. Are you facing temptation? Approach the throne of grace with confidence. Are you discouraged? Approach the throne of grace with confidence. Are you burnt out due to standing up for the truth? Approach the throne of grace with confidence.

We very much need His help if we are going to boldly and passionately live for Him. If you want to fight the good fight, run the race, and keep the faith, you must go to God for help. You cannot rely on your own strength. Luckily, you can approach the throne of grace, with God waiting there, ready to provide you with mercy and grace in your time of need.

Reflection Questions:

How do I view praying for God's help? Am I eager to ask for God's help, or is it my last resort?

Why am I able to approach God's throne of grace with confidence?

What are some things that I need God's help with? How will my prayer life look different in the coming weeks?

New Testament in 60 Days: Luke 18-19, Eph. 3-4

Day 28 - God Desires Your Sanctification

For this is the will of God, your sanctification
- 1ˢᵗ Thessalonians 4:3

One desire many Christians have is to know the will of God for their lives. I know that this is a desire I have as well. A few times in Scripture, we are graced with a plain statement of what God's will is for us. This is one such place, and we find that the will of God is for us to be sanctified.

What does God want for your life? He wants the flesh to weaken and the spirit to flourish. He wants you to be conformed to the image of His Son. He wants you to become more like Christ every single day. He wants you in close communion with Him. The process of these things becoming a reality is called sanctification. This process often brings struggle and hardship. It is no light and easy task to become sanctified. It often involves painfully ripping sin out of your life. It often involves realizing that many things you enjoy are full of sin and need to be abandoned. It often involves humbling yourself time and time again to ask the Lord for help.

Because of this, many Christians do not want to be sanctified. They may say that they want to be conformed to the image of Christ, but their hearts say something else. They want to hold onto their music full of sinful lyrics. They want to watch their sexually explicit TV shows. They want to be unwise and ungodly in their romantic relationships. They don't want to admit that they need His help.

If the will of God is that we are sanctified, who are we to tell Him no? If the will of God is that we remove sin from our lives, who are we to tell Him that He is wrong? If God appeared to you visibly, talked to you audibly, and told you what needed to change in your life, would you change? You likely would. After all, God told you Himself. What difference does it make if God tells us in person, or through His Word? God tells us to flee from sin and be set apart for Him, multiple times in His Word. Each of those instances are just as authoritative as if God Himself appeared and spoke to you audibly. God speaks about our need for sanctification all throughout His Word. We would do best to listen, especially if we are passionate about living for Him.

Reflection Questions:

What does it mean to be sanctified?

How do I feel about being sanctified? Am I willing to embrace the difficulty that accompanies sanctification?

In what areas of my life do I need to pursue sanctification? Is it my thought life, my speech, my relationships with others?

New Testament in 60 Days: Luke 20-21, Eph. 5-6

Day 29 - Be Perfected By The Spirit

Are you so foolish? Having begun by the Spirit, are you now
being perfected by the flesh? - Galatians 3:3

In the battle for your life and your sanctification, you
cannot win by yourself. Our modern era is full of self-help
videos, motivational speeches, and training regimens that have
convinced us that it is in our power to do anything we set our
minds to. While this may be true for things such as exercise,
healthy sleep habits, and discipline with studying, it is not true
in the realm of sanctification.

Sanctification is God's work. Yes, we seek to implement
godly habits in our lives. Yes, we obey what He calls us to do.
Nonetheless, we cannot sanctify ourselves. We cannot pretend
that the efforts of the flesh can purify the flesh. I cannot clean
dirty dishes with a dirty sponge. I need something more. It is
the same with sanctification. Sin is waging war against you. The
flesh is waging war against you. The world is trying to drag you
down, and the devil wants you to complacently embrace sin.
Do you really think that your own efforts can conquer all of
those foes? No! You need God.

It is ironic how many will preach that salvation is entirely
through Christ, then believe that sanctification is entirely
through us. While we don't preach works-based salvation,
many of us believe in works-based sanctification. If we are
struggling with lust, we must beat it by our own strength. If we
are struggling with swearing, we must kill the habit by our own
power. If we have anger issues, the only one who can fix it is
us. In the war against sin, we forget that we need Him.

Now, it is not as though we sit around and wait for God to magically remove all sinful desires and temptations. We must live in surrender to Him and follow wherever He leads. We are not sanctified simply by behavioral modification, but through the inner transformation done by the Holy Spirit. Many Christians believe that the goal of sanctification is modified behavior. Set up enough boundaries, set up enough healthy habits, read enough books, and sin will no longer be tempting. Those practices are not wrong, and I encourage all Christians struggling with a specific sin to take appropriate steps to distance themselves from it, yet inner transformation is needed that can only come through God. In fighting the good fight, we must begin and continue in the Spirit, never believing that we can be perfected by the flesh.

Reflection Questions:

What are some sins that I have tried to defeat on my own strength? Do those battles feel hopeless?

How do I view my role in sanctification? Am I called to beat sin, to sit around, or to be obedient to God's calling as He works?

Have I viewed sanctification as a matter of behavioral modification, or inner transformation?

New Testament in 60 Days: Luke 22-24, Phil. 1-2

Day 30 - You Have An Enemy

Be sober-minded; be watchful. Your adversary the devil
prowls around like a roaring lion, seeking someone to devour
- 1ˢᵗ Peter 5:8

You have an enemy; someone whose primary goal is to destroy your faith and cripple your walk with God. That enemy is Satan. The Bible says that he is like a roaring lion, always on the watch, waiting for an opportunity to pounce on the perfect victim. You may be shocked at this. Why would anybody seek to destroy you, a simple college student, banker, parent, etc.? It is because you have aligned yourself with God. When you ally yourself with Christ, His enemies become yours.

Satan does his best work when we are unaware that he is on the prowl. When we are mindful and watchful of his tactics, then his effectiveness is severely diminished. When we stop paying attention to spiritual things, that is when he strikes. The enemy is constantly looking for opportunities to attack you. He is looking to cripple your spiritual growth. He is desiring to tempt you with sin. He wants to make the things of God unappealing and the things of the world appealing. His primary goal is your destruction.

When someone knows that they have an enemy fighting against them, they prepare. When an enemy nation would raise an army against ancient Israel, Israel would raise an army as well. When Germany started taking over parts of Europe, England began wartime preparations. Likewise, we must prepare against the enemy of our souls. As Satan is waging war against us, it would be foolish to sit around and pretend like this enemy does not exist. It would be ignorant to believe we are so insignificant that Satan would never make time for us. God cares about every eternal soul, including yours. Satan does as well.

An awareness of our enemy is the first step in defeating him. If we know that Satan is against us, we are more likely to press into prayer and the Word. We are more likely to pursue the things of God, knowing there is a constant effort by the devil to drive us away. Satan is a defeated foe and will be forever thrown into the lake of fire, but that does not stop him from causing chaos in the here and now. Let us be on guard and realize that he is severely weakened if we know that he is coming.

Reflection Questions:

How do I feel knowing that I have an enemy who is dedicated to my destruction?

Am I typically one who is indifferent toward spiritual discipline? How does the knowledge of Satan's goals change my attitude towards the things of God?

What are some things I can do on a daily basis to guard myself against Satan's efforts to derail my faith?

New Testament in 60 Days: John 1-2, Phil. 3-4

Day 31 - Provide No Opportunities

Give no opportunity to the devil - Ephesians 4:27

Do not provide Satan any opportunity to impact your life. One of his primary goals is your destruction. He cannot hurt your salvation, but he can hurt your sanctification. He can hurt your spiritual discipline. He can hurt your marriage, your friendships, and your familial relationships. Do not give him that opportunity. Do not give him the opportunity to sneak sin into your life.

This is why one verse earlier Paul says, "do not let the sun go down on your anger" (Ephesians 4:26). He knew that unchecked anger is an opportunity for Satan. Unchecked pride is an opportunity for Satan. Unchecked jealousy is an opportunity for Satan. Satan can fuel these emotions in order to push us toward sin. Unchecked anger can turn into rage, which is then taken out on our loved ones. Unchecked pride can grow into heavy arrogance that causes us to act recklessly. Unchecked jealously can developed into deep resentment, destroying any gratitude we have toward God. Satan wants those things to happen. Do not give him the opportunity to use unchecked emotions for evil.

Furthermore, do not give Satan the opportunity to tempt you. Many Christians, though they love God, live around much more sin than they should. They watch shows that contain explicit content. They listen to music with unholy lyrics. They surround themselves with friends who live for the world. All of these are opportunities for Satan to tempt us. When an explicit scene appears, Satan wants us to watch instead of skip. When ungodly lyrics are playing, he wants us to sing along, singing words we would never otherwise say. When our friends partake in sin, Satan wants us to go along and partake as well.

Any opportunity that Satan has, he will use. Do not give him such opportunities. Living for God is difficult, and it means having the devil as your enemy and adversary. If we want to live for God, to advance His kingdom, and to fight the good fight, we must not give Satan any opportunity to turn us away from that calling.

Reflection Questions:

What opportunities have I provided Satan in the past? What opportunities am I currently providing him?

When was a time that an avoidable sin or temptation spiraled out of control? What could I have done to avoid that sin in the first place?

How does my mindset surrounding my actions change knowing that Satan will take full advantage of every opportunity I give him?

New Testament in 60 Days: John 3-4, Col. 1-2

Day 32 - God Will Establish You

But the Lord is faithful. He will establish you and guard you against the evil one - 2nd Thessalonians 3:3

The Christian life involves many battles. One of these battles is against the devil, as we have been previously reading about. He wants to make our world increasingly wicked. He wants sin to fester in our lives and wants to weaken our faith. As we engage in this battle, we must remember that it is not fought alone. On his own, Satan is an intimidating foe. Who am I to stand against the leader of the opposition against God, the chief demon, the prince of the power of the air? If I were put in a fight against Satan, I would lose 100 times out of 100. I cannot stand against him on my own.

Yet, I am not standing alone. I am not left to contend on my own against the forces of hell. I am allied with the King of Kings and the Lord of Lords. And it is the Sovreign of the universe that promises to establish me and guard me against the evil one. If God is the one who is holding me up, who could possibly destroy me? If God promises to guard me against Satan, what could Satan possibly do? He may try to scare me, send demons against me, or tempt me, but God is with me. Satan is a defeated enemy. He knows that he has lost, and that his eternal destiny is in the lake of fire experiencing God's judgment. He is simply trying to do as much harm as possible before his inevitable defeat.

Many Christians have developed an unhealthy fear of Satan. They view him as an existential threat to their existence, someone who could strike at any moment to destroy their faith and send them to hell. While Satan is most definitely a threat that we should be aware of, he is nothing in comparison to God. If you are fearful of the devil, press into God. If you want to stand firm against the devil, press into God. God will surely establish you and guard you, keeping your soul safe.

Reflection Questions:

What do I think about the devil? Do I view him as irrelevant, as a threat, as a fatal enemy?

Do I underestimate how Satan can attack me and impact my faith? Do I overestimate his abilities?

How can understanding God and His nature take away any fear I may have of the enemy?

New Testament in 60 Days: John 5-7, Col. 3-4

Day 33 - Total Abstinence From Evil

Abstain from every form of evil - 1ˢᵗ Thessalonians 5:22

From an overarching view, the life of the Christian is in many ways a battle between good and evil, between God and the devil, between sin and holiness, between truth and lies. We struggle against sin in our lives. We fight that the devil would lose his grip on those who are not saved. We persevere so that God's glorious truth will triumph over lies.

Because of this, it is important that we not only abstain from evil in a broad, general sense, but abstain from every individual form of evil. There are many "small" or "minor" forms of evil that we embrace in our everyday lives. We may scoff at the idea of doing drugs yet sing along to songs about drugs and alcohol. We may gasp at the prospect of extra-marital sexual activities yet glue our eyes to the screen at characters in our favorite movies and TV shows partaking in that very thing. We completely reject the idea of murdering an individual, but for our enemies, we make every effort to slander them and kill their reputation. We often assume that because a sin is "smaller" or "less evil," that somehow makes it acceptable or good.

Evil will take different forms. Sometimes, it will even disguise itself as good. Think of "reproductive rights" and "sex positivity," which are simply attempts to make what is evil appear as though it were good. Sometimes, evil will hide itself behind a lack of consequences. Lusting after someone else often has no immediate consequences, so we rationalize that it must be alright. Similar logic often follows for drinking, cursing, and more. No matter the evil, we must abstain from it. Whether it is "small," marketed as good, or considered harmless, it is still evil.

If we are going to whole-heartedly follow God, if we are going to run the race set before us, we must abstain from every form of evil. All of us have our "pet" sins, those sins in our lives that we really enjoy. They are sins we think aren't too bad or aren't taking us away from God. Friend, every sin takes us away from God. Let us abstain from every form of evil, knowing that we are called to holiness in every area of life, major or minor.

Reflection Questions:

What are some evils that I am allowing in my life or excusing?

How have I seen evil take the form of something "minor"? How have I seen evil take the form of something good?

What evil do those around me often partake in? How does it market itself?

New Testament in 60 Days: John 8-9, 1st Thes. 1-2

Day 34 - Walk By The Spirit

But I say, walk by the Spirit, and you will not gratify the desires of the flesh - Galatians 5:16

This is the key to following God and running the race set before us. Walk by the Spirit every day. Spend every day closely in-tune with God and relying on the Holy Spirit. We often start our day with God and end our day with God, yet God is not present throughout our day. I once spoke with a group of men who told me their plan for triumph over habitual sin. In every situation that could bring about temptation, they would pray. They would instantly go to the Lord in prayer and ask the Holy Spirit for supernatural strength and transformation of their desires. These men knew that they must not only start and end by the Spirit but had to take every step by the Spirit.

Later in Galatians, Paul tells us that "if we live by the Spirit, let us also keep in step with the Spirit" (Galatians 5:25). We walk by the Spirit by keeping in step with Him. We should not call on the Holy Spirit once in the morning and once at night, but all throughout the day. The flesh is always present in our lives. We cannot escape it, for sin is a part of our human nature. If the flesh is a consistent presence, why do we not make reliance on the Holy Spirit consistent as well?

It is one thing to struggle with sin. It is another thing to struggle with sin while never relying on the Spirit. Many Christians are confused as to why sin has taken such a deep hold in their lives, yet they are prayerless, never in the Word, and never being built up by other believers. They truly want sin out of their lives, yet God is not a consistent part of their lives. The flesh cannot be conquered by our own will power.

It is only beaten by the power of the Holy Spirit. The more you listen to the Holy Spirit, the less you will listen to the flesh. The more you cling to God, the less that sin will cling to you. If you want to fight the good fight of the faith, you must walk by the Spirit.

Reflection Questions:

> Am I someone who walks by the Spirit, or occasionally calls upon Him?

> Do I typically call upon God when facing temptation? Why or why not?

> What are some ways that I can walk by the Spirit throughout my day?

New Testament in 60 Days: John 10-11, 1st Thes. 3-5

Day 35 - Who Are Your Friends?

Do not be deceived, "Bad company corrupts good morals"
- 1st Corinthians 15:33

Be very careful who you surround yourself with. In the Christian life, your contemporaries are of the utmost importance. Is your life full of those who encourage you as you chase after Christ? Do your friends cheer you on as you stand for truth? Does your inner circle uplift you and support you in your battle against sin? No battle is fought alone. No soldier goes into combat by himself, but has an army with him. This army offers community, encouragement, and support as everybody pursues the same objective. A strong group of godly men and women functions the same, providing support and encouragement as each person chases after God. Serving and living for Him is much easier with godly men and women by your side.

Nobody wants to go into battle with those who are apathetic, cowardly, or indifferent. The Christian life becomes much harder when everyone around you has surrendered to sin and stopped caring about the truth. Spreading the good news becomes quite burdensome if your peers have become indifferent to the eternal fate of those around them. There is a heavy weight placed on your shoulders when those around you are apathetic to the things of God. It is even more burdensome when those around you are actively opposed to God and His ways. That is why we are warned that bad company corrupts good morals. Ungodly friends will negatively impact your life and drag you away from God.

We are also told to not be deceived regarding this truth. Many think that they can spend every day in the house of corruption and not become corrupt. Many think they can surround themselves with scoundrels and not become a scoundrel themself. Many are deceived into believing that they could never be influenced negatively by those around them. That is simply not true. Our friends influence us much more than we believe, for better or for worse.

Man of God, woman of God, be careful who you are surrounding yourself with. Surround yourself with those who will support you in the fight and who are also in the fight themselves. It is much better to chase after God alongside other godly men and women, rather than those who want nothing to do with Him. If your inner circle rejects the call to follow Christ, you will soon do so as well.

Reflection Questions:

What types of people am I surrounding myself with?

Are my friends pushing me towards Christ? Are they pulling me away from Him?

What are some godly friendships I should invest in more?

What are some ungodly friendships I need to pull away from?

New Testament in 60 Days: John 12-14, 2nd Thes. 1

Day 36 - Suffering Should Be Expected

For it has been granted to you that for the sake of Christ you should not only believe in Him but also suffer for His sake, engaged in the same conflict that you saw I had and now hear that I still have - Philippians 1:29-30

Philippians is often considered a letter of joy. Many people view it as a friendship letter between Paul and the church is Philippi. Tucked in this letter of joy is Paul's warning to the church, that they are not destined to simply believe in God, but also suffer for Him. Not only that, but they will have the same conflict that Paul is currently engaged in.

Engaged in the same conflict as Paul? That sounds terrible! Paul was beaten, arrested, hated, driven out of towns, and multiple attempts were made on his life. It is somber for Paul to suggest that the Philippians would encounter similar hardship. Paul's conflict came from following the call to spread the truth of Christ and live a holy life pleasing to God. Following this call brought suffering. The church in Phillipi would suffer in following that call, and we will as well.

Be mindful of the fact that Paul did not command the Philippians to seek out suffering or conflict but wrote that these things have been granted to them. Suffering and conflict are a part of following Christ. Friend, if you are reading this and say "yes, I believe in Jesus," then you are simultaneously taking a stand against the world, against the flesh, and against the devil. That is a conflict you are voluntarily entering. That is a conflict that will bring suffering.

Because of this, we should not be surprised when we suffer. Peter tells us to "not be surprised at the fiery trial when it comes upon you to test you, as though something strange were happening to you" (1st Peter 4:12). We should not view suffering as out of the ordinary, being taken off guard when it arises. Rather, we should expect it. When you accept that suffering for Christ is a part of the faith, life becomes a lot easier. One of the worst parts of suffering is being caught off guard by it, yet we will not be caught off guard when suffering for Christ. The King of Kings and the Lord of Lords was crucified by this world, so why would we expect to follow Him and suffer no harm?

Reflection Questions:

> What are some ways that following Christ creates conflict with the world?

> What is my attitude towards suffering for the faith? Do I expect it, or am I caught off guard?

> Am I willing to suffer and endure hardship for the sake of Christ? Why or why not?

New Testament in 60 Days: John 15-16, 2nd Thes. 2-3

Day 37 - Expect Persecution

Indeed, all who desire to live a godly life in Christ Jesus will be persecuted - 2nd Timothy 3:12

If you want to live for Christ, you will be persecuted. This one of the hardest truths for Christians to grasp. We ignore it. We overly emphasize the positive aspects of faith. We do everything we can to avoid this important truth. If you want to live for Jesus, you will suffer. You will be attacked. The world will fight against you. The devil will be against you. The powers that be will come against you. You will be persecuted. The Christian faith stands anti-thetical to the sinful world that we live in. It should be no surprise that the sinful world will seek to crush the faith as a result.

Luckily, if you are okay with the truth about persecution, the Christian life becomes much easier. If you are unprepared for persecution, it will catch you off guard and hurt even more. You will be taken aback, wondering why anybody would hate you for your Christian faith. If you understand that following Christ inevitably leads to persecution, you will be well prepared for the battles ahead.

It is important that we understand that only those who desire to live a godly life will be persecuted. Very rarely are people persecuted for believing that Jesus is real. The world will not come against you for saying "I follow God." They will come against you for actually following God. This is one of the biggest ways to distinguish between those who are fighting the good fight and those who are sitting on the sidelines. Those who live their life for God will receive criticism and persecution. Those who claim Christ without living for Him will largely remain untouched.

Those in the early church were well acquainted with persecution. Christians in the first few centuries after Jesus' death were hunted down, martyred, mocked, and more. In some parts of the world, Christians still suffer the same fate. Yet, despite all the persecution these men and women of God suffered, Christ was worth more. Persecution is nothing compared to the love of God and the eternal promise of the gospel.

Reflection Questions:

Am I desiring to live a godly life, or am I sidelining my faith?

Do I expect to experience persecution for my faith or does the concept seem foreign to me? Why or why not?

How can the hope of the gospel help me endure persecution?

New Testament in 60 Days: John 17-18, 1st Tim. 1-2

Day 38 - Suffering Over Sinful Pleasure

By faith Moses, when he was grown up, refused to be called
the son of Pharoah's daughter, choosing rather to be
mistreated with the people of God than to enjoy the fleeing
pleasures of sin - Hebrews 11:24-25

Moses was used by God because he was willing to suffer. He had a choice: enjoy a comfortable life of luxury, living among the rulers of the land, or suffer alongside God's people who were living as slaves. It is one thing to have suffering suddenly come upon you, but it is another thing to choose it. And that is what Moses did. He would rather suffer for God than live in sinful luxury.

Christians must all make a similar choice. Will you live a comfortable life pursuing meaningless pleasure, or live for God? One promises you ease and comfort, while the other promises you purpose, meaning, and eternal rewards. Moses was willing to embrace suffering for the sake of obeying God's call on his life. He could have remained royalty and eaten the finest foods, had sexual relations with the most beautiful women, and worn the most expensive clothes. He could have had a life full of fun, pleasure, and comfort. He likely experienced a lot of that before he fled into the wilderness. Nonetheless, he was willing to give it all up for God.

The sinful world will always try to distract you from pursuing God's call on your life. It will try to entice you with comfort, drag you down with meaningless pleasure, and offer you something "more enjoyable" than living for God. The world will offer you the comfort of living for yourself, the pleasure of hedonistic indulgence, and the "freedom" of not being accountable to God. For many, that is too tempting to turn down. Yet, we must say no to the fleeting pleasures of sin if we are to faithfully serve God.

Many Christians want to have both. They want the meaning and purpose that comes from following God, with the pleasures and comfort of embracing the world. Trying to have a foot on each side on the fence will never work and leave you unsatisfied and unfulfilled. You must choose one or the other. If you want to fight the good fight, to serve God all of your days, you must choose God over the pleasures of sin. You must be willing to chooser godly suffering over sinful comfort.

Reflection Questions:

If I were Moses, would I have given it all up to serve God and identify myself with His people?

What sinful pleasures do I have a hard time letting go of?

Do I want to live a life of meaningless ease or one of purpose? Which life am I living right now?

New Testament in 60 Days: John 19-21, 1st Tim. 3-4

Day 39 - The World Will Hate You

Do not be surprised, brothers, that the world hates you
- 1st John 3:13

One of the strongest desires for many is the desire to be liked. We all want people to like us, to think good things about us. It is much nicer to be liked than to be hated. We are often taken by surprise when someone doesn't like us. We search frantically through our minds, trying to figure out the source of their distaste for us. Is it the way we talk? Is it our outfit choices? Is it our opinion on certain things? Once we discover why an individual dislikes us, we often try to remove that factor in order to gain their favor and approval.

This tendency, though, must cease when it comes to Christianity. The world will hate us. There should be no surprise about that. The world is sinful yet self-righteous, wants to live for its own pleasures, and does not want to own up to the consequences of its actions. Christianity says that we all are sinners, that we should live for God above all else, and that we will be held accountable for how we live. The Christian faith is the antithesis of the sinful ways of the world. Because of this, hatred and dislike are inevitable.

While we may change aspects of ourselves to be liked by others, we cannot abandon our faith or compromise on the truth to gain the approval of others. To follow Christ means to be hated by the world. That is a truth we must accept. Embracing that truth, though, provides us with an unprecedented amount of freedom. If I am okay with being hated for the sake of Christ, hatred cannot catch me off guard, deter me, or push me away from following Christ. It cannot sway me from my beliefs. If standing with Christ means standing against the world, so be it. I would rather have the acceptance of Christ and the rejection of man than the rejection of Christ and the acceptance of man. I would rather boldly follow Christ, accepting the hatred of the world, than abandon the faith to win the world's favor.

Reflection Questions:

Have I personally been hated by the world for my faith? If not, what are some parts about my faith that I would likely receive hatred for?

Does the world's hatred of Christianity surprise me? If so, what made me expect that Christianity would be loved by the world?

How does the acceptance of Christ change how I view the hatred of man?

New Testament in 60 Days: Acts 1-2, 1st Tim. 5-6

Day 40 - Press On

I press on toward the goal for the prize of the upward call of God in Christ Jesus - Philippians 3:14

Press on, friend, press on. Be like Paul, who did not stop. He kept pushing forward, moving past every adversity. He wrote that "three times I was beaten with rods. Once I was stoned. Three times I was shipwrecked; a night and a day I was adrift at sea" (2nd Corinthians 11:25). You would think that those hardships would have stopped him. After the first few beatings, you would guess that Paul would say, "I need to stop." You would bet that suffering so greatly and immensely would have taken him out of the race. He could have rationalized his choice to quit and say, "I did enough, it is time for me to stop." But he never did. There was no point in time where Paul would ever say, "I can stop serving God." Prison couldn't stop him. He sang hymns and evangelized to jailers. Storms couldn't stop him. He preached to the men aboard the ship. House arrest couldn't stop him. He wrote letters to churches and ministered to those who visited him. Paul was unstoppable. Upon encountering hardships, he simply said, "I press on."

Why did he press on? What kept him going? He knew that the work he did was of eternal significance. He was not working for an employer, for his own personal gain, or to witness a more prosperous Rome. He was laboring for God. He wanted the prize of the upward call of God. He was passionately following what God had called Him to do, and serving His King was the ultimate prize.

It can be easy for Christians to cave when hardship strikes. We lose friends after standing up for our faith and resolve to never stand up for Christ again. We lose sleep one night while staying awake to pray, and our fatigue makes us say, "this is too much to do again." We are bold for Christ once, suffer as a result, and decide that since we defended the truth once, we have done all that we need to. Christians are becoming increasingly content with saying, "I suffered for God in the past, I do not have to any longer." If that is you, heed the words of Paul. Press on. When hardship comes, press on. When trials come, press on. When persecution comes, press on. May serving your Lord and Savior be the ultimate prize, and may you press on in pursuit of that prize.

Reflection Questions:

How do I feel after reading about Paul's hardships? Am I surprised that he didn't quit after suffering so much?

What motivates me to take action in my day-to-day life? Is it my friends, family, a boss, etc.? Is the service of God a strong or weak motivator for me?

How willing am I to press on through adversity?

New Testament in 60 Days: Acts 3-4, 2nd Tim. 1-2

Day 41 - You Are Not Alone In Your Struggles

The same kinds of sufferings are being experienced by your
brotherhood throughout the world - 1st Peter 5:9

You are not alone. You are not alone in your struggle
against sin. You are not alone in your experiences of
persecution. Your battle is not unique to you. As a Christian,
that truth fill you with joy. You are not alone in what you are
experiencing. Our struggles worsen when we believe that we
are all alone. When we struggle with a habitual sin, our shame
is multiplied when we start to believe that nobody else
commits that same sin. When we face persecution, we can
encounter a crushing sense of hopelessness if we believe that
there is nobody else standing up for Christ.

Loneliness is one of the greatest discouragers as a
Christian. Feeling alone in a sin struggle, feeling alone in
persecution, feeling alone in standing for Christ, all push us to
give up and to stop trying. Those battling sin, when feeling
alone, may give up the fight and allow that sin to take over.
Those under persecution may renounce Christ if it seems as
though no one else is standing with them. Those fighting for
the truth may stop speaking out if they believe that they are
the only active voice.

Whenever we have thoughts that tell us we are alone, we
must return to this truth from 1st Peter. You are not the only
one struggling with that specific sin. There are many other
Christians struggling with it as well, even if they don't speak
about it. You are not the only Christian being persecuted. All
across the world, there are many suffering for Christ. You are
not the only one standing up for the truth. There are bold

individuals, many of whom will never be widely known, that are fighting in their city, on their college campus, at their church, etc.

If you are feeling alone, hopeless, and as though you should give up, know that you are not alone. Find other believers to talk to. They have likely had similar experiences to you, no matter how unique or obscure you think your situation is. Godly men and women, if you seek them out, have the powerful ability to encourage you, uplift you, and let you know that you are not alone. Living for God can be discouraging, and running the race is especially exhausting if you believe you are all alone. Know that you are not.

Reflection Questions:

In what ways do I believe that I am utterly alone? Is it in a specific sin, persecution for my beliefs, losing friends, or something else?

Am I encouraged knowing that many people are fighting the same battles that I am? Why or why not?

Who are some men and women of God that I can turn to in order to feel less alone?

New Testament in 60 Days: Acts 5-7, 2nd Tim. 3-4

Day 42 - Be Strong In The Lord

Finally, be strong in the Lord and in the strength of His might - Ephesians 6:10

The Christian's source of strength is God. The battle in front of us seems looming and impossible. There is a battle over our sanctification and holiness. There is a battle over the eternal destinies of those around us. There is a battle over the truth, which is consistently distorted and buried under endless lies. These battles may be impossible for us, yet they are not impossible for God.

Mighty men and women of God throughout history did not achieve great things by their own strength. They did not muster up enough courage, have a strategic enough plan, or have enough wealth to fund their projects. They relied on God and His strength. They said, "I cannot do it, but God can do it through me."

Throughout the Bible, there were many battles fought. Joshua conquered Jericho and sought to defeat the Canaanites. David rose up against Goliath. Israel was constantly at war with the surrounding nations. Whenever these battles happen in Scripture, it is often noted that God fought the battle for Israel, that God delivered the enemies into Israel's hand. Israel fought, yet God's strength was the deciding factor. How else could a previously nomadic group of freed slaves defeat some of the strongest nations in the world? It was only through the strength of God.

That is why we must be strong in the Lord and the strength of His might. If we rely on our own strength, we will inevitably fail. We may achieve small victories on occasion, but our path will be full of defeat, despair, and discouragement. As Christians, we are fighting against the world, the flesh, and the devil. Those are impossible foes for a measly human being to defeat. Can we really defeat sin on our own? Can we really change the sinful world by ourselves? Can we really shine a light into the hearts of others by ourselves, even though Satan works nonstop to blind them? We can't.

If you want to boldly live the Christian life, if you want to fight the good fight, you need God's help. This does not revoke our responsibility to show up and serve Him, but is rather a call to rely on God's strength instead of believing that we can do it on our own. Do not be strong in your own abilities, but in the Lord and the strength of His might. To fight the good fight, we need Him.

Reflection Questions:

What battles do I face as a Christian? Do they seem too difficult or impossible to win?

Do I tend to rely on my own strength or God's in my faith journey? How has that been helpful or hurtful?

Am I willing to rely on God's strength for the Christian life, or am I clinging to the futility of doing it all myself?

New Testament in 60 Days: Acts 8-9, Titus 1-2

Day 43 - God's Abundant Comfort

For as we share abundantly in Christ's sufferings, so through
Christ we share abundantly in comfort too
- 2nd Corinthians 1:5

What should be no surprise at this point is the fact that following God will bring suffering. If you truly want to fight the good fight, it will be difficult. Luckily for us, God does not leave us to suffer. He will not let us remain permanently in our pain and discouragement. God promises to comfort and uplift us along the way. His Word says that if we partake in suffering for Christ, we will partake in comfort as well.

God knows the difficulty that comes from following Him. He is not surprised or taken aback to see His people suffer for His sake. God knows that suffering will occur, which means He also knows we need comfort. The Bible says that "the Lord is near to the brokenhearted and saves the crushed in spirit" (Psalm 34:18). Christians are often brokenhearted and crushed in spirit. When we suffer for Christ, it is easy to wallow in our misery. We can spend all our time and energy feeling sorry for ourselves and lamenting over our pain, forgetting that God is the ultimate comforter. He knows exactly what we need and exactly how to soothe our hearts.

In painful situations, it is normal to seek comfort. We go to our friends for support. We give ourselves a treat to cheer us up. We engage in a relaxing activity. What many Christians fail to do is turn to God. It seems as though God is our last resort for comfort, while He is by and large the best comforter. When a child gets hurt, they often run to their parents for comfort and support. A child with a skinned knee will run to their mom or dad, yearning for a hug and reassurance that everything will be okay. If children run to their parents for comfort, we should run to our heavenly father for comfort. If we start turning to God when we suffer, not as a last resort but as our first resource, we will be much better equipped to live for Christ and endure suffering, knowing that we have the ultimate comforter on our side.

Reflection Questions:

What are some ways that I suffer as a Christian?

What things do I normally turn to when I suffer for Christ? How effective are they at comforting me?

Is God my first source of comfort or my last resort? Why?

New Testament in 60 Days: Acts 10-11, Titus 3, Philemon

Day 44 - Rejoice, Pray, And Give Thanks

Rejoice always, pray without ceasing, give thanks in all circumstances; for this is the will of God in Christ Jesus for you - 1ˢᵗ Thessalonians 5:16-18

Here, we encounter another place in Scripture where we are told the will of God for our lives. In many ways, this is the trio for thriving in the midst of the battles of faith. Fighting for our sanctification, for the souls of those around us, and for the truth, is tiring. It brings discouragement and weariness. To imagine a whole life spent in this battle can almost be too much to bear. Yet here, we read amazing wisdom that will help us thrive.

First, we are told to rejoice. Joy counteracts sadness, weariness, and discouragement. As Christians, we are to be joyful. Now, joy is different from happiness. Happiness is temporary and comes from temporal events and circumstances. I am happy when I get a bonus at work, when my favorite team wins, or when I eat a good meal. Joy, contrarily, is based in something foundational and unwavering. I have joy because the King of the universe died for my sins, and I have the opportunity to live for Him. When you face sadness and discouragement in the Christian life, think of your King who humbled Himself and died so that you could spend a joyful eternity with Him.

Secondly, we are told to pray without ceasing. If our aim is to live for God and serve Him, then it is important that we spend time with Him. Prayer refreshes us. It restores our spiritual vigor and our hope in God. That is why Paul tells us "do not be anxious about anything, but in everything by prayer and supplication with thanksgiving let your requests be made known to God" (Philippians 4:6). When we pray, we give God our burdens and anxiety, receiving His peace in return. This is something that must be done often if we are to remain strong when fighting the good fight.

Finally, we are told to give thanks in all circumstances. Bitterness hinders us from living out God's will. When we are bitter, we sit in our frustration, letting our emotions fester rather than taking action. Bitterness, if left alone for too long, can also lead us to sin against others and God. Bitterness is beaten by gratitude. By being grateful, by giving thanks in all circumstances, our bitterness will melt away. How can we be bitter at God and others when He has given us so much to be thankful for?

Reflection questions:

Is my life void of joy? What are some eternal truths I can focus on to fill me with joy?

How consistently do I pray? Will my prayer habits change knowing that prayer is a command from God?

How often do I give thanks for the things in my life? What would consistent gratitude look like for me?

New Testament in 60 Days: Acts 12-14, Heb. 1-2

Day 45 - Prayer Works

The prayer of a righteous person has great power as it is
working. Elijah was a man with a nature like ours, and he
prayed fervently that it might not rain, and for three years
and six months it did not rain on the earth. Then he prayed
again, and heaven gave rain, and the earth bore its fruit
- James 5:17-20

One of the truths that has changed my prayer life, and is
likely to change yours, is that prayer works. Now, every
Christian I know believes in their mind that prayer works, but
not many believe in their heart. They pray with an attitude of,
"maybe God cares and maybe He will do something." Because
of this, they pray half-heartedly and on spurious occasions. To
fight the good fight, we must make prayer a foundational habit
of our lives and believe that there is power in prayer.

Look at Elijah. He was one singular man, standing against
the evils of Ahab and Jezebel. He prayed that it would not rain.
He prayed, and prayed, and prayed. And God answered him!
Because of Elijah's prayers, it did not rain in Israel for three
and a half years. Imagine what that would have been like, with
it all happening because of one man's prayers.

As John Knox was fighting to bring the Protestant
Reformation to Scotland, he prayed and told God, "Give me
Scotland, or I die." His mighty prayers paved the way for
Presbyterianism in Scotland. "Bloody" Queen Mary of
Scotland was recorded as having said "I fear the prayers of
John Knox more than all the assembled armies of Europe."

There are countless other examples of the power of
prayer. Joshua prayed that the sun would not set for a day, and

it didn't. With a prayer, Samson regained his strength to take down the Philistines. Hannah prayed for a son, and the nation of Israel was blessed with Samuel. Friend, prayer works. God responds.

Now, I am not implying that every prayer will be answered on the spot, or even in the way that we want it to be answered. Rather, I simply seek to demonstrate that God hears our prayers, He cares about our prayers, and He often acts in response to our prayers. This knowledge should encourage us, bolster our faith, and help make fervent prayer a regular part of our lives.

Reflection Questions:

How would believing in the power of prayer change my prayer life?

Do I believe that God cares about my prayers? I may say I believe, but do I truly?

How can the stories of Joshua, Hannah, Elijah, and more, encourage me to pray fervently and often?

New Testament in 60 Days: Acts 15-16, Heb. 3-4

Day 46 - Don't Avenge Yourself

Beloved, never avenge yourselves, but leave it to the wrath of
God, for it is written "Vengeance is mine, I will repay" says
the Lord - Romans 12:19

Just because you are living for God does not mean that
you will never experience anger. People will hurt you. People
will mistreat you and do wrong to you. It is inevitable. If you
are actively standing for God and against the world, the
chances of this happening increase dramatically. In all of this,
it is easy to become vengeful. We want to get back at those
who hurt us. We want to stick it to them, to ruin their
reputation, to make them feel the pain that we did. We believe
that acting in our anger is the righteous thing, yet "the anger
of man does not produce the righteousness of God" (James
1:20). When we try to make things right, to settle the score
ourselves, we often do more harm than good. We often
unnecessarily hurt others out of our wrathful anger.

Even more painful that being hurt, though, is when people
hurt us and get away with it. When wrongdoing is done, we
always feel better if the culprit gets the justice they deserve. A
desire for justice is natural and healthy. Yet, if the offender
receives no justice, it can be crushing. These instances make
the victim feel helpless and hopeless. One can only think of
the Soviet Union, which horribly abused its citizens for
decades. Many of these tormentors never received justice for
their evil acts.

Know that God is the ultimate judge and that He will
enact justice. God will make sure every wrongdoing is paid for,
as He is the only one who can implement perfect justice.

Unlike humans, who are flawed and let greed, anger, and other sin get in the way of actual justice, God's implementation of justice is perfect. We can rest knowing that He will bring judgment upon every sin. When evil occurs in the world and seems as though it goes unopposed, know that God will judge it. When people deeply hurt us, and it feels as though nobody is holding them accountable, know that they will have to answer to God. Sleep well knowing that every wrongdoing will be paid for, either in hell or on the cross. As you fight the good fight, you do not need to worry about avenging yourself. This is not a call to inaction in the face of injustice, letting atrocities occur unopposed. Enacting justice is important for a flourishing society and holding people accountable is definitely biblical, but remember that ultimately, vengeance is reserved for the Lord.

Reflection Questions:

Have I ever been hurt by someone who got away with it? How does that make me feel?

Do I feel hopeless about the state of justice in our world? Does it seem like evil occurs unopposed?

How do I feel knowing that God will enact perfect vengeance? Does that give me any sense of peace or hope?

New Testament in 60 Days: Acts 17-18, Heb. 5-6

Day 47 - Destroy Arguments

We destroy arguments and every lofty opinion raised against
the knowledge of God, and take every thought captive to
obey Christ - 2nd Corinthians 10:5

In today's world, many people view differences in ideas
and beliefs as merely differences in opinion. Christians can
unfortunately fall into the same trap. We believe one gospel,
others believe a different one, that is okay. We believe marriage
is one way, others have a different opinion. We don't believe
that certain views are correct or incorrect, but simply a
difference in personal preference.

That is not the approach Paul took. For him, truth was
never a matter of opinion. Truth is one of the biggest
battlegrounds in our day and age. Postmodernism has
convinced many that morality is relative. The sexual and
gender revolution has destroyed any notion of a God given
design to humanity. False teachers have distorted the gospel
into something unrecognizable. Truth is under attack, and we
must defend it.

We must destroy arguments and lofty opinions that set
themselves up against God. We must fight for the truth. Moral
relativism declares that we are the determiners of right and
wrong, not God. Are we going to stand against that? Gender
theory and the sexual liberation movement laugh at any notion
of a God given design for marriage and sexuality. Will we let
that stand unopposed? Liberation theology has made
Christianity into temporal, earthy religion as opposed to a
heavenly one. Have we decided to let it run free?

We must examine ourselves and our reaction to lies. Are we angered by them? Do we detest them? Do we even care that these lies exist? Are we pained to see people disregard right and wrong? Does it hurt to witness God's design become perverted? Do we have any anger at seeing false teachers spit on the glorious gospel of our Lord and Savior?

The world is launching a full-frontal assault against the truth of God, truth that is near and dear to our hearts. Are we willing to fight back? When something you care about is under attack, you rush to defend it. You would never watch as your family member is assaulted, as your friend is slandered, or your house is being burnt down. God's truth is important and we should care about it. Because of that, we should not idly sit by when it is under attack. When the world raises arguments and lofty speculations against the knowledge of God, let us stand up and fight for our Lord and King.

Reflection Questions:

What is my reaction when people slander God and His truth?

Do I feel any desire to stand up for the truth of God?

What are some ways in my everyday life that I can destroy arguments and lofty opinions that oppose God?

New Testament in 60 Days: Acts 19-21, Heb. 7-8

Day 48 - Avoid Shipwreck

Wage the good warfare, holding faith and good conscience.
By rejecting this, some have made shipwreck of their faith
- 1st Timothy 1:18-19

If you are to live the Christian life, if you are to wage the good warfare, you will need to hold onto faith and good conscience. Put differently, you must have right belief and right living.

Hold onto faith. Hold onto right belief. To have any quality of faith, you must be believing the right things. You cannot hold onto heresies and wrong beliefs about God. Of course, none of us will have 100% correct theology. We will all get to heaven and learn what we were wrong about during our time on earth. Nonetheless, there are fundamental beliefs of the faith that must not be compromised.

Friend, if you deny core doctrines of Christianity, such as the virgin birth, the resurrection of Christ, the substitutionary atoning death of Christ, and more, your faith is bound to suffer shipwreck. Whenever key beliefs of the faith are abandoned or twisted, the rest of one's faith is bound to crumble.

Secondly, we must have good conscience. In our minds, we must be set on doing the right thing. Too often, Christians will hold the correct beliefs, then discard any notion of right and proper living. There are those who profess all the right things, then live for the world. For those who act this way, they will also suffer a terrible shipwreck of faith. It is impossible to profess that you are a sinner humbly seeking the forgiveness of the Savior, then intentionally pursue sin. The cognitive dissonance will cause one side to win out over the other. Either you will abandon your reckless pursuit of sin or abandon your faith.

As we live this Christian life, as we fight the good fight, we must hold onto faith and good conscience. We must believe the right things, avoiding heresy, and have our hearts set on living for God instead of the world. If we do otherwise, if we abandon faith or good conscience, then we should not be surprised when our walk with God deteriorates into oblivion.

Reflection Questions:

How does proper belief help me follow Christ? How does proper living impact my relationship with Him?

Is there any way I have "lost" faith? What about a good conscience?

How can I better orient my mind to the truth about Christianity and about how I should live?

New Testament in 60 Days: Acts 22-23, Heb. 9-10

Day 49 - Contend For The Faith

Contend for the faith that was once for all delivered to the saints - Jude 3

There is a battle against Christianity, and surprisingly, this battle is often waged within the church. While those outside of the church will try to discredit Christianity, there are many bad actors within the church that subtly try to distort Christianity and strip it of its saving power. These are the false teachers that are warned about in the Bible and are the focus of Jude's epistle.

In response to these false teachers, we are called to contend for the faith. We are not supposed to sit on the sidelines and hope that things work out. For many Christians, they see false teaching, see the truth being twisted, and do nothing about it. They carry on with their life and hope that somebody else will deal with the issue. While false teachers are quick to enter the battlefield in order to spread their lies, many Christians are quick to leave the battlefield and hope that someone else will rise to defend the truth.

Friend, you are called to contend for the faith. This does not mean that you pursue endless battles for the sake of being combative. Rather, it means that you refuse to be idle while lies are in your midst. If your friends hold false beliefs, lovingly correct them. If those close to you are being fed spiritual lies, provide them with the truth. If people in spiritual authority are promoting heretical views, oppose those views however you can. If there is nothing you can do directly, pray that the truth would prevail and train your discernment so that you can better detect lies.

There are too many Christians who see false teaching, who see lies being spread, and refuse to do anything about it, whether that be pray, speak up, etc. Unfortunately, in the battle for the faith, identifying lies without countering them is just as effective as indifference. Contending for the faith may seem intimidating. We may worry that we do not know enough, do not have enough credentials, or are not articulate enough. If that is you, fear not. As Christians, we are not called to success, but to obedience. When we take a stand for the truth, God takes our efforts much further than we could ever imagine.

Reflection Questions:

What are some popular lies that circulate among Christians?

Have I ever contended for the faith? What pushed me to do so, or what has been holding me back from doing so?

Where are some areas in my life where I can contend for the faith? My friend group? My school? My household?

New Testament in 60 Days: Acts 24-25, Heb. 11-13

Day 50 - Do Not Yield

To them we did not yield in submission even for a moment,
so that the truth of the gospel might be preserved for you
- Galatians 2:5

Paul did not yield. He did not compromise. There was no surrender. The gospel was the hill that Paul was going to die on. During this period in history, the gospel was under attack from the Judaizers. While the message of Christ was repent and trust in Him, the message of the Judaizers was repent, trust in Him, and observe the rules and regulations of Judaism.

Paul knew that this seriously corrupted the gospel and destroyed any power that it had to save. So, when the opportunity came to stand up for the truth, Paul did not yield and confronted the Judaizers head on. For many Christians today, that would be too confrontational. They would desire to "build bridges" and "seek areas of common ground." While there are definitely non-essential doctrines that can be disagreed on, the gospel is not one of them. Distorting the gospel is heresy, and we do not build bridges with heresy.

We must adopt that attitude of Paul. No compromise. No surrender. We must be willing to defend the truth and die on the hill of the gospel. We cannot compromise with liars and heretics to preserve a false sense of peace and unity. We must care more about the gospel than false unity.

The temptation to compromise on truth will always be present. Compromising promises comfort, less tension, and one less battle that you have to go through. If you want ease in the Christian life, compromise is way the to achieve it. God's truth will always be at war with the thoughts and opinions of this world. If you hold to God's truth, you are voluntarily entering a battle that will not cease until Jesus comes back. That is a battle you must be okay fighting. Otherwise, you will compromise and turn your back on God. Let us adopt the mindset of Paul, who never yielded, especially when it came to the gospel.

Reflection Questions:

What are some Christian beliefs that are currently under attack by the world?

What are some ways that I have compromised on the truth, or been tempted to?

What are some consequences that can come from compromising on the truth?

New Testament in 60 Days: Acts 26-28, James 1-2

Day 51 - The Need For Apologetics

Always being prepared to make a defense to anyone who asks you for a reason for the hope that is in you - 1st Peter 3:15

Why do you believe what you believe? Why do you believe that Jesus was who He said He was? Why do you believe that only He is the way, the truth, and the life? Why do you believe that the resurrection of Christ happened, as opposed to being a cleverly devised myth? It is important that you not only know what you believe, but why you believe it as well. We live in a society full of skepticism. People are often unwilling to accept a proposition at face value. When we try to evangelize and share Christ with others, they will not simply accept what we say as truth. They will want to know why it is true. When you start learning not just what is true, but why it is true, you have entered the realm of apologetics.

Many Christians are scared by the word "apologetics." They think that apologetics is for those with doctorates, or those who have endless hours of study available to them. That is not true. Apologetics is for every Christian. It is important that you understand why you believe what you believe, because those close to you will not look for answers given by the top apologists, those with PhD's, etc. They will bring their questions to you.

This seems like a heavy burden, and it is. Nonetheless, this does not mean that you must pursue an advanced degree or make apologetics your sole hobby. It simply means that you must have a defense for the faith. You must be able to give an answer, a real answer. "That's just what I was told" is not an answer. "I feel like it is true" is not an answer. As Christians, we must be able to give a real answer when questioned about why we believe what we do. These answers do not have to be overly technical or complicated, but they must properly "give a reason for the hope that is in us."

Learning apologetics will strengthen our own faith as well. Many Christians have problems with doubt because they do not know why they believe what they believe. A faith without reason will be torn about by doubt. If left unanswered, even silly questions such as "how do I know Jesus even existed" can deal a deadly blow to one's faith. If you understand why you believe what you believe, you will be better prepared to defeat doubt. If you desire to learn apologetics, start today! Investigate reasons for the existence of God. Learn about the evidence for the resurrection of Christ. Study why Christianity is true as opposed to other religions. The task of learning to make a defense is one that will strengthen us and help us fight the good fight ahead of us.

Reflection Questions:

Do I know what I believe and why I believe it?

If someone asked me why I believe in Christianity as opposed to other religions, what would I say?

What do I think about defending the faith? Is that something I can do with confidence?

New Testament in 60 Days: Rev. 1-2, James 3-4

Day 52 - Blinded Minds

In their case the god of this world has blinded the minds of
the unbelievers, to keep them from seeing the light of the
gospel of the glory of Christ, who is the image of God
- 2nd Corinthians 4:4

Satan works non-stop to prevent people from coming to
Christ. That is a truth you must realize. That is why the Bible
says he blinds the minds of unbelievers. Satan does not want
them to know God. Just as we are engaged in a spiritual battle,
unbelievers are also engaged in a spiritual battle, even if they
do not know it.

Unbelievers are unaware, but there is an enemy of their
souls who never ceases to wage war against them. Satan and
his demons spend 24 hours of every day making sure that your
friends and family do not come to know God. Satan is fighting
endlessly to make sure that those around you go to hell. Now,
this does not change the fact that people are sinful and have a
natural aversion to the things of God. The unbelief of
individuals is not Satan's fault, it is entirely their own.
Nonetheless, we must know that Satan labors to keep people
in this unbelief and stop the light of the gospel from ever
reaching their eyes.

Would that knowledge change how we act? Would that
knowledge change how we pray? Would that knowledge
change how we evangelize, or see the need to evangelize? If
Satan fights every day for our loved ones, why don't we fight
every day in prayer? If Satan fights every day for people to
believe lies, why don't we seek to speak the truth however we
can?

Are we truly going to let Satan fight harder than us? Are we truly going to sit passively as he seeks to further his grip on those we care about? When we get to heaven, we will know and understand much more than we do right now. It would be a tragedy if we got to heaven and realized that Satan cared far more about the souls of our loved ones than we did. In fighting the good fight, we are not just fighting for our own sake, but for the sake of those around us. Let us realize that Satan is fighting as well.

Reflection Questions

Who in my life needs a saving knowledge of Christ?

How strong is my desire to see my loved ones saved? Is it strong or mild?

How does understanding Satan's war on unbelievers impact my worldview? How will it change how I live?

New Testament in 60 Days: Rev. 3-4, James 5

Day 53 - Expose The Deeds Of Darkness

Take no part in the unfruitful deeds of darkness, but instead
expose them - Ephesians 5:11

It is obvious that there is great evil in the world. Internet
pornography is one of the biggest economic industries of the
day, with much of its content being produced using women
who are trafficked. Young children are being given life-altering
synthetic hormones to "fix" gender dysphoria that often isn't
there. Teenage girls are receiving double mastectomies on a
whim, as doctors interpret "I am uncomfortable in my body"
as "I am a boy and want my breasts removed." No-fault
divorce rips apart families on a whim, as selfish spouses decide
that they are simply not enjoying marriage enough to keep
going. False teachers sneakily lead people astray, using sweet-
sounding lies to send others on the path toward hell.

There is a lot of evil in the world, and we are called to
expose it where we can. Yes, Christian reader, it doesn't matter
who you are. You are called to expose evil. In Nazi Germany,
Dietrich Bonhoeffer led an association of churches that spoke
out against the evils of the Nazi regime. There were 3000
churches allied with Bonhoeffer, 3000 allied with the Nazi's,
and 12000 that chose not to side either way. These "neutral"
churches were opposed to the Nazis but assumed that they
should just focus on Jesus and let everything else sort itself out.
They did not want to expose the unfruitful deeds of darkness.
Overpowered due of the indifference of the "neutral"
churches, those allied with Bonhoeffer were silenced by the
Nazis, and the voice of the church against evil was
extinguished.

Many Christians are afraid to speak out against evil because they fear the social consequences. Yet, it is better to be ostracized for opposing evil than to be included for remaining indifferent to it. Other Christians may think that their voice is unable to accomplish anything. They view their voice as so small that it could never make a difference. Yet, our calling is not to have success, but to stand for God and stand against evil. We are called to obedience, not results. We must believe that God will find a way to use our obedience and our speaking up, even if we don't understand how He could.

Reflection Questions:

Besides what was listed, what other "deeds of darkness" are common in the world today?

Have I remained silent in situations when I should have spoken up?

Do I remain silent because I believe that my efforts will be pointless? How does understanding our call to obedience rather than results change my mindset?

New Testament in 60 Days: Rev. 5-6, 1st Peter 1-2

Day 54 - A Harvest Will Come

And let us not grow weary of doing good, for in due season
we will reap, if we do not give up - Galatians 6:9

Friend, do not grow weary. The battle is long and arduous. The fights for your soul, the world, and the truth are fought every single day. Do not grow weary. It is proper for Paul to use the example of reaping a harvest. Harvests take a long time. Seeds are planted and watered, but no progress is seen for months. Then all of a sudden, the plants sprout. Across the field, the crops flourish and the farmer receives his bountiful harvest. Yet, it was the consistent faithfulness of the farmer that brought about this harvest. He did not grow weary. Day by day he watered the plants. Even though there were no visible results at first, he was not discouraged. He knew the harvest was coming.

If we keep doing good, we will reap a harvest as well. It will take time, yet we should not stop. Our prayers may not be answered for months or even years, yet that does not mean we should cease to pray. The fight against habitual sin can take years, yet that does not mean the fight is worthless. Memorizing Scripture may seem futile at first, yet a treasury of knowledge is built up after years of faithfulness.

It is quite easy to grow weary in doing good, especially when we don't see results. It can seem as though our efforts are going to waste. We water the seeds day after day, and it appears as though the only thing we are doing is wetting the ground. If we were farmers, many of us would give up, believing our efforts to be futile. It is much easier to accept the futility of a few days of effort than discover years later that our work was futile. Yet, our work in doing good is not futile. Though the ground we water does not change, seeds are sprouting under the surface. We may sow seed and water the plants, but God gives the increase. Our effort to do good, whether that be in prayer, evangelism, battling sin, or something else, goes further than we may believe. God often uses our efforts in ways we could not imagine. As Christians, our calling is not to see results, but to be faithful. And if we are faithful, we will one day see the harvest.

Reflection Questions:

What seeds am I trying to sow? Have I gotten weary of doing good?

Have I ever seen a harvest in my life? How long did it take until I saw the results of my faithfulness to God?

How do I feel knowing that God uses my efforts in ways I don't often see or understand? Is that encouraging? Will it help me "not grow weary in doing good"?

New Testament in 60 Days: Rev. 7-8, 1st Peter 3-4

Day 55 - Fan Your Gift

For this reason I remind you to fan into flame the gift of God - 2nd Timothy 1:6

You have a gift from God. I do not know what it is. It could be preaching. It could be writing. It could be music. It could be art, or hospitality, or medicine, or service. No matter what it is, you have been uniquely gifted in a way that allows you to serve God and advance His kingdom. Do not waste that gift. As Paul commands Timothy, fan into flame that gift.

Timothy was gifted in many ways. He was an excellent leader, pastor, and defender of doctrine. Paul did not want these gifts to go to waste. In a similar fashion, make sure that your gifts don't go to waste. There are too many wasted gifts in this world. Friend, do not be a gifted failure. There are too many individuals who have been gifted and empowered by God, then squander their gift. It could be because they are distracted by meaningless pursuits. They may be using their gifts to build their own personal kingdom. They may simply lack the confidence needed to step forward and pursue God's call. You do not know what great things God can do through you and your gifting, so don't ignore it.

Now, your vocational work does not have to line up with your gifting. You may be a skilled preacher, but that does not require you to serve in pastoral ministry. You may be talented at composing music for the glory of God, but that does not mean you need a job as a worship leader. Too many Christians believe that their gifts can only be exercised in a career setting, then abandon their gifts until said career comes around. You do not need a paid job to fan your gifts into flame. You do not need "the perfect opportunity" to grow the gifts God has given you. The time is now. You may have the opportunity to preach, but you can lead a Bible study with friends. You may not have the opportunity to publish worship music, but you can volunteer at your local church. Your art may not be in a museum, but that shouldn't stop you from painting and teaching others to do so. God is powerful enough and sovereign enough to know how to use our gifts for good, even if we believe that He cannot.

Reflection Questions:

What are some ways that God has uniquely gifted me? How can these gifts be used for His kingdom and for His glory?

Have I been ignoring the gifts that God has given me? Have I been waiting for the "perfect opportunity" or the right vocation?

What are some ways I can use my gifts that I might not have previously thought of?

New Testament in 60 Days: Rev. 9-11, 1st Peter 5

Day 56 - Some Go Before, Some Follow

The sins of some people are conspicuous, going before them to judgment, but the sins of others appear later. So also good works are conspicuous, and even those that are not cannot be hidden - 1st Timothy 5:24-25

God sees. He sees the work you put in. He sees your striving and laboring for the kingdom of God. God sees, He knows, He cares, and He will reward you. And God also sees all sin. Sin done in full view, and sin done in the dark. Paul writes about how some sins are evident, while others come to light later. For some, their sin has instant consequences. Others have consequences that fail to appear until years later. Some sins are so obvious when committed that they are on display for all to see. Some sins are hidden from the public eye until they are finally uncovered later in the future. Yet, whenever sin may come to light, and whatever its earthy consequences are, God sees every sin and will punish every sin. Every sin in the world will be judged and punished by God, with judgment being placed either on the sinner or on Christ on the cross.

Good works follow a similar pattern. Some good works are evident to all. Others are done for no applause. Some good works reap an instant reward. Other seeds take years and years to finally sprout. Nonetheless, God sees every good work. If nobody else sees your efforts, God does. And be sure that God will reward you for every good work. Good works cannot be hidden forever. They will either be made known in this life, or the life to come. Your labor is not hidden, it is not forgotten, it is not unappreciated. God sees, and He cares.

God is the ultimate judge. He is the ultimate vindicator. It can be easy to see the wicked prosper, the righteous suffer, and become nihilistic about the state of the world. It can be discouraging to work tirelessly for the Lord's sake and receive no acknowledgement or recognition. Many Christians give up, throw in the towel, and complain that God truly must not care about the good they do, or the evil done by others. If that is you, or has been you in the past, remember that God sees and cares. There is no good deed that will go unrewarded, and no sin that will go unpunished. That should give us the confidence to boldly serve Him every day, to fight the good fight, with or without recognition from others. Remember, though we enter the good fight, the battle is not over until we are with Christ again. It is at that time when all the scores will be tallied.

Reflection Questions:

Is it frustrating to see people get away from wrongdoing? How does that knowledge of God's eternal judgment impact how I feel?

Have I ever felt as though my good works were pointless? Was it because of a lack of recognition?

How can God's place as the all-knowing Sovereign of the universe be an encouragement as I live for Him?

New Testament in 60 Days: Rev. 12-13, 2nd Peter 1-2

Day 57 - I Can Do All Things

I can do all things through Him who strengthens me
- Philippians 4:13

Besides Jeremiah 29:11, this may be the Bible verse that is the most misquoted, the most often taken out of context. Typically, when this verse is used, it is used in the context of a personal goal. "I can get this promotion through Christ. I can win this competition through Christ. I can improve this skill through Christ." That is the improper way to view this verse and was not Paul's intent. A verse earlier, Paul wrote that "I know how to be brought low, and I know how to abound. In any and every circumstance, I have learned the secret of facing plenty and hunger, abundance and need" (Philippians 4:12).

Paul sets up his confident declaration in Philippians 4:13 by speaking about his life circumstances. He has been popular and hated. He has been well fed and gone hungry. He has been rich and poor. He has known ease and luxury, as well as pain and discomfort. After speaking about the variety of circumstances he has endured, Paul says "I can do all things through Him who strengthens me." He can face any situation through Christ. He is not speaking about achieving personal goals and desires, but about enduring hardships and faithfully serving God.

This truth is extremely important for us today. When following God, we will inevitably encounter obstacles that are too difficult for us, that loom over us and seem impossible to overcome. We may encounter financial hardship, lose friends while standing up for Christ, or leave our job over Christian convictions. These are situations we can face with Christ. What is impossible for man is easily possible for God. If we try to face difficult and overwhelming circumstances on our own, we will inevitably become burdened and beaten down. If we rely on Christ, we are not promised an easy victory, but we do know that we can do all things through Him who strengthens us. That should give us the confidence and boldness to fight the good fight, knowing that through Him, we can face whatever comes our way.

Reflection Questions:

What are some difficult circumstances that I am facing?

What challenges have I been trying to face with my own strength and abilities, when I truly need to be relying on God?

Am I willing to admit that I need God's help, or is my pride stopping me?

New Testament in 60 Days: Rev. 14-15, 2nd Peter 3

Day 58 - The Promise Of Future Glory

For I consider that the sufferings of this present time are not
worth comparing with the glory that is to be revealed to us
- Romans 8:18

"You only live once." That is a message spread far and wide throughout our culture. It is used as a rallying cry for secular thought. You get one life, then you die. You might as well make the most of it. Have as much fun as possible. Make as many friends as possible. Live a life maximizing your enjoyment. This mindset makes people adverse to hardship and suffering. After all, if I only get so many years on this planet, why would I voluntarily fill them with pain instead of pleasure?

This mindset has unfortunately affected the church as well. Many Christians' primary concern is their own enjoyment and personal quality of life. Many are unlikely to voluntarily suffer for the sake of Christ, because they are of the mindset that it would be a waste of their one precious life.

Paul masterfully defeats this mentality in the book of Romans. When considering the sufferings of this present life, he points to eternity. If you are a genuine Christian, you are promised a glorious eternity with God. You are promised endless lifetimes in which you can know God, rejoice in Him, have fun, and so much more. I cannot even explain how amazing eternity with God will be, because any description I give is bound to fall short. God's promised eternity is far better than anything my mind could imagine.

If we keep eternity in mind, we become much more willing to suffer for Christ's sake in this lifetime. What are grueling missions trips, late nights spent in prayer, rejection for the sake of Christ, and any other suffering you could imagine, in comparison to an eternity with God? This is not to say that we are not allowed to enjoy this life. God gives us many things to enjoy. Friendships, food, nature, sex, etc., are all amazing gifts from God to us. Rather, it is to say that we should not be averse to suffering for Christ. We should not look back on our lives and say, "I wish I served God less and had more fun." God promises us a million lifetimes of a gloriously amazing eternity with Him and with other believers. What is a lifetime of suffering for His sake in comparison to that?

Reflection Questions:

Have I fallen into the "you only live once" mindset? Has that gotten in the way of serving God?

Have I ever regretted serving God because it got in the way of something that I wanted to do?

How does having an eternal mindset change how I view this life? Does it change my willingness to serve God and suffer for His sake?

New Testament in 60 Days: Rev. 16-17, 1st John 1-3

Day 59 - A Christian Soldier's Call

Be watchful, stand firm in the faith, act like men, be strong
-1st Corinthians 16:13

Here we read a series of commands like those that would be given to a soldier entering battle. First, be watchful. Be aware of the battle. Soldiers cannot go into battle with wandering minds and drifting attention. The battle requires their full attention. The spiritual fight requires ours. While we do not have to spend all of our mental energy on the things of God, we must be aware of that we are fighting the good fight and that it is fought every single day.

Secondly, stand firm in the faith. Soldiers must be confident in what they are fighting for. Any Roman soldier not sold out for Rome was bound to flee at the first sight of danger. Know what you are fighting for. You are seeking to serve and advance the kingdom of the King of Kings and the Lord of Lords, the one who died for your sins, and will come back to judge the living and the dead. Do not waver from that commitment.

Third, act like men. Soldiers could not go into battle acting like a young child. Young children are undisciplined, have little resolve, and cave to fear. Men in battle must steel their minds, strengthen their resolve, and realize that they are fighting for something greater than themselves. We must do the same. This is not just applicable to men, but women as well. As Christians, we must embolden ourselves and develop a strong resolve to serve Him. We cannot fight the good fight acting like a child.

Finally, be strong. Soldiers must be strong in battle. Strength in battle is much more mental than it is physical. It is the strength to push past difficulty, to do the hard but necessary things, and to not give up. In the Christian life, we must be strong as well. We must endure hardship, do difficult things when needed, and never give up, always pressing on toward the goal of the upward call of Christ.

Solider of Christ, you are fighting the good fight. Be watchful, stand firm, do not act like children, and be strong. Be ready to serve your God and King at all times.

Reflection Questions:

Am I watchful in regards to my spiritual life? Am I aware of the quality of my faith?

Do I stand firm in the face of opposition? Do I compromise on my faith when persecution occurs?

Am I bold in my faith? Am I sold out for God in all that I do, or does my commitment waver?

Do I persevere in faith? Do I have strength when it comes to the things of God, or do I fall apart when struggles arise?

New Testament in 60 Days: Rev. 18-19, 1st John 4-5, 2nd John

Day 60 - Labor On

Therefore, my beloved brothers, be steadfast, immoveable, always abounding in the work of the Lord, knowing that in the Lord your labor is not in vain - 1st Corinthians 15:58

I love this charge of Paul to the church in Corinth. Stay the course, do not be shaken, always pursue the work of the Lord. The church would have a massive impact on the world if every Christian adopted this mindset. One reason people are hesitant to adopt this mentality is because they think that their work is in vain. They are steadfast, immoveable, abounding in God's work, but it seems as though they are not making a difference. When our efforts appear to be worthless, the naturally human tendency is to stop putting in effort. If that is you, please know today that your labor in the Lord is not in vain.

It can be discouraging to think our efforts have gone nowhere. Our prayers are not answered. The mountain of sin feels staggeringly high. Those around us seem hopelessly lost. It is this discouragement that often causes Christians to stop serving the Lord with boldness and zeal. They give up and assume that all they have done is in vain. Friend, I implore you to remain steadfast. Nothing done for the Lord is wasted. It would be wrong to believe that we can serve God to no effect. He will use whatever we give Him. No prayer is wasted. No conversation is wasted. No reading of the Word is wasted. Pursuing the things of God and serving Him will always be worthwhile, even if solely for the fact that it sanctifies us and draws us closer to Him.

In following Christ, there will be many instances in which we cannot see the fruit of our faithfulness. We will not always be able to see the fruit of our labor. Remain steadfast, nonetheless. Be immoveable, nonetheless. Our calling is to be faithful rather than to see results. Fortunately, when we reach heaven, we will see the fruit of all our labor. Nothing you do is in vain. Nothing is wasted. Fight the good fight. Finish the race. Keep the faith. Labor on.

Reflection Questions:

Am I someone who gets easily discouraged? Does this inhibit me from serving God to my fullest extent?

Do I ever feel like my service of the Lord is all in vain? What makes me feel that way?

How do I feel knowing that God can use every action of service done for Him? Will that change anything about how I live?

New Testament in 60 Days: Rev. 20-22, 3rd John, Jude